GiANNi HAVER
MiX & REMiX

SWiSSNESS
iN A NUTSHELL

Bergli Books
...feel at home in Switzerland

Illustration Credits
u = upper, b = bottom, c = centre, l = left, r = right
p. 25b: © Karlen Sattlerei und Handels GmbH
pp. 29, 44ul, 44bl, 60u, 72, 73, 84ul, 108ul, 108ur, 122b: © Bibliothèque de Genève
p. 42u: © Archives Laténium Neuchâtel
p. 43: © Cantonal Fine Arts Museum, Lausanne – photo J-C. Ducret
p. 44c: © Heinz Baumann, Altdorf
pp. 45, 46u, 61u, 84, 123cr: all rights reserved
p. 46b: ©2011 STUDIO100 MEDIA
p. 61b: © Michel Kichka
p. 74b: © Claude Jaccard / Vaud-photo
p. 84: © Swissmint (coin)
p. 85b: © Light Art Gerry Hofstetter – Photo François Vittoz
p. 96b: © Swisscom
p. 97: © Peter Nicholson
p. 111: © Swiss National Library, Bern
p. 123ul: © Private collection, Lötschental Museum
p. 123u: © Musée de l'Elysée, Lausanne

Every attempt has been made to correctly credit the legal owners of all images
in this book. Please contact us if you feel you have been overlooked.

Acknowledgements by the translator
My special thanks go to Gordon Read for his eagle-eyed editing, and to Heidi,
Raphaël and Felicia for their patience in proofreading.

First published in French as *L'Image de la Suisse*
Copyright © Editions Loisirs et Pédagogie SA, Le Mont-sur-Lausanne. 2007.
www.editionslep.ch

English edition translated from the French by Robert Middleton
Copyright © 2014 Bergli Books, an imprint of Schwabe AG, Basel, Switzerland
www.bergli.ch

Printed by: Schwabe AG, Muttenz/Basel
Printed in Switzerland

ISBN 978-3-905252-65-1

Contents

Institutions

External relations

Index

Foreword

The image we have of a country is not uniform. It comprises many ingredients, all of which have strong symbolic value; some are concrete (visual images, like landscapes) – others are more abstract (mental images, such as the supposed characteristics of the population). This little book explores these various aspects which, together, make up the image of Switzerland: an image that characterises the country abroad but also – and above all – makes it unique in the eyes of its inhabitants.

The image of Switzerland is not immutable. It is in constant evolution, and the elements that it comprises are often inter-related and interdependent. Our choice of subject-matter – and its presentation – is only one approach among others, and aims to provide the reader with some key ideas that may help understand why the components of Swissness have become part of national identity.

At the end of each chapter, some specific pictorial examples are included to support and give depth to the subject-matter itself. These include postcards, posters and various items, some less expected than others, some even surprising – they reinforce the subject-matter and give it a footing in reality.

An interest in the foundations of national identity makes it easier to understand what makes Switzerland what it is today – to wonder at it or perhaps try to encourage it to evolve.

Introduction

Overview map
Some concepts

Overview map

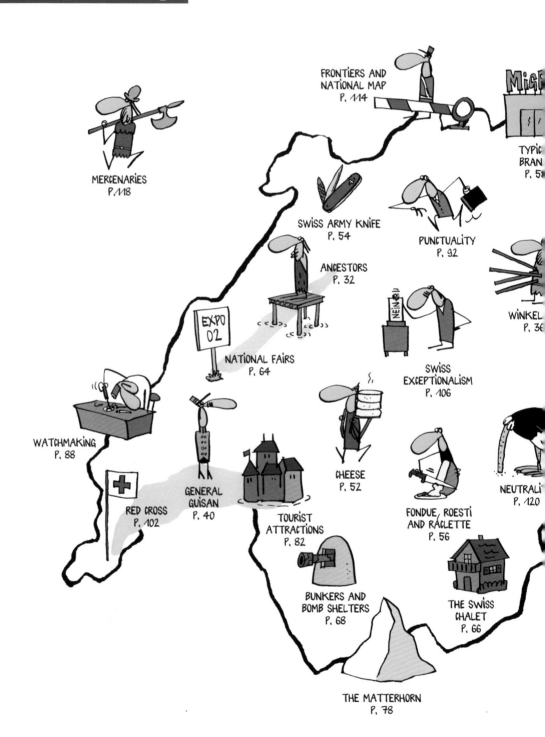

FRONTIERS AND
NATIONAL MAP
P. 114

Migr

TYPIC
BRAN
P. 5

MERCENARIES
P. 118

SWISS ARMY KNIFE
P. 54

PUNCTUALITY
P. 92

ANCESTORS
P. 32

WINKEL
P. 36

EXPO
02

NATIONAL FAIRS
P. 64

SWISS
EXCEPTIONALISM
P. 106

WATCHMAKING
P. 88

CHEESE
P. 52

NEUTRALI
P. 120

RED CROSS
P. 102

GENERAL
GUISAN
P. 40

TOURIST
ATTRACTIONS
P. 82

FONDUE, ROESTI
AND RACLETTE
P. 56

BUNKERS AND
BOMB SHELTERS
P. 68

THE SWISS
CHALET
P. 66

THE MATTERHORN
P. 78

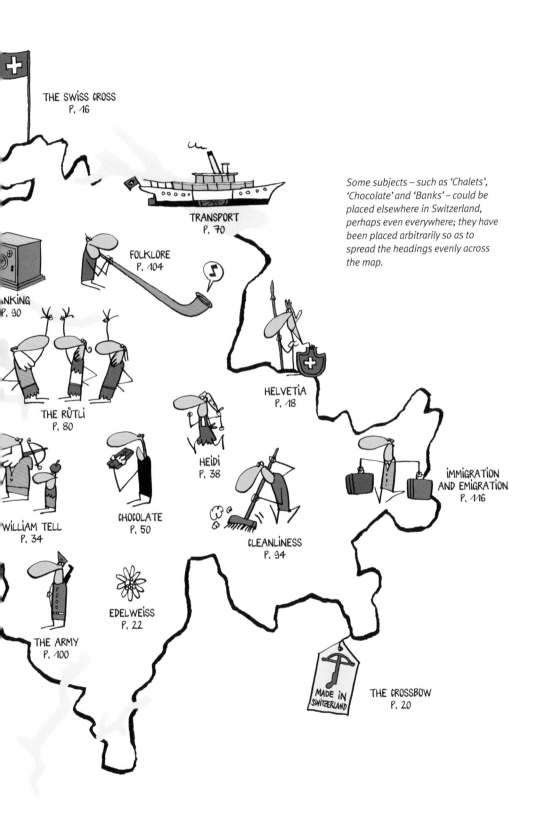

THE SWISS CROSS
P. 16

TRANSPORT
P. 70

FOLKLORE
P. 104

Some subjects – such as 'Chalets', 'Chocolate' and 'Banks' – could be placed elsewhere in Switzerland, perhaps even everywhere; they have been placed arbitrarily so as to spread the headings evenly across the map.

...NKING
P. 90

HELVETIA
P. 18

THE RÜTLI
P. 80

HEIDI
P. 38

IMMIGRATION
AND EMIGRATION
P. 116

WILLIAM TELL
P. 34

CHOCOLATE
P. 50

CLEANLINESS
P. 94

THE ARMY
P. 100

EDELWEISS
P. 22

MADE IN
SWITZERLAND

THE CROSSBOW
P. 20

Some concepts

The concepts presented here help explain the components of 'Swissness' and how they are sometimes linked.

Images and representations

- A **physical image** is first and foremost an object (a painting, a poster or a photo, for example); but it only gains its full significance in relation to another object, person, situation etc. (not usually present), of which it is the **representation**.

  An image never represents reality in full. Choices – aesthetic, ideological etc. – intervene in its composition and some aspects are given greater prominence than others. Reality is 'filtered' and the image is never neutral, never objective.

- In day-to-day life, visual, aural and emotional information is stored. The mind processes this information as **'mental representations'** that provide the basis for understanding images and enriching them with elements that are not actually 'in' them.

  Mental representations not only make it possible to recognise a fire in a photo of a fire; they also allow the photo to evoke warmth, the smell of embers and memories linked to evenings at the fireside – even to sense other connotations, pleasant or not.

- Some representations are shared by a group of people, large or small. These are **social representations**. If they are well anchored in the collective imagination, they allow members of the group to interpret certain images in the same way.

  If the fire shown in the photo mentioned above is the bonfire of the 1st of August (Swiss national day), these social representations allow the Swiss not only to recognise it as such, but also to associate values with it – such as patriotic feelings – which are not linked to their own individual experience, but to their membership of a group (in this case, inhabitants of Switzerland).

In 1929, René **Magritte** (1898–1967), the Belgian surrealist painter, created a famous work entitled 'La trahison des images' (The treachery of images), showing a pipe with the caption 'This is not a pipe.' In this way, Magritte pointed out that – even if it is very realistic, as in the case of the pipe – a picture is not identical with the object that it represents. 'This is not a pipe' but the image of a pipe, as proven by the fact that you can't smoke it.

THIS IS NOT A PIPE !

The collective imagination

- Thanks to a faculty that is specific to humans: **imagination**, we create and organise mental representations. It allows us to go beyond the simple **perception** of things – we can classify them, put them in order or give them a meaning, positive or negative.

- Imagination is **individual**. It allows us to create and maintain our own **imaginary resources**. However, our relationship to the outside world is also determined by the society in which we live. In this way, imagination can be placed in a wider, **collective** context. Taking this into account, we can define the contours of the collective imagination.

  Analysis of images produced by a group is one of the best methods for defining the collective imagination at a given moment.

- Images and collective imagination stand in dual relationship. The latter allows members of a group to interpret images, but, in turn, the images thus interpreted reinforce the development of the collective imagination **every day**.

  During a campaign to make it easier to deport non-Swiss criminals, an image of a black sheep being kicked out of a group of white ones was used in a poster by the right-wing political party SVP. Since then, at least in the German-speaking part of Switzerland, a picture of a sheep carries more complex connotations in the collective imagination than before.

- Defining, controlling and influencing the collective imagination is vital for the exercise of power. The collective imagination is thus of central importance **in politics**.

National Identity

- National identity comprises a series of **points of reference shared** by people belonging to the same **national community**.

- These shared points of reference can be **real** – all inhabitants of Switzerland live in a confederation, for example; or **widely believed** – the Swiss are descended from the Helvetians *(Helvetii)*, for example.

- The State concerns itself with the definition of these shared references and with planting them in the popular mind, in schools and public service media. The **sense of belonging**, linked to national identity, is fundamental to the **internal cohesion** of a country.

In Switzerland, there are two pivotal moments in the development of national identity:

– in 1848, when the modern State was founded: everything that promoted unity between the confederated parties was given prominence in order to shift their sense of belonging from their canton towards the new Confederation;

– from the 1930s and during the second World War: in order to stand up to the powerful ideologies that dominated neighbouring countries, a policy was initiated by the authorities and subsequently promoted by the media and other cultural milieux, which was known as 'spiritual national defence': it emphasised everything that was typically Swiss, to the point that some historians treat it as retrograde nostalgia.

Some concepts

'Myth', 'culture', 'stereotype' and 'symbol' are terms in everyday use, but their content is richer than might be supposed from the way they are normally used.

The myth

- In current usage, a myth is a false **belief**. For those interested in images, symbols and national identity, it is not relevant whether a myth is 'real' or not.

  William Tell never existed – yet the myth about him has an impact on Swiss identity.

THE GREAT MYTHS:

OEDIPUS TELL

I WANT TO KILL MY FATHER!

- A myth is a **story**, frequently of oral origin and **widely shared**, that makes it possible to explain or make sense of the existence of a group.

  A myth is described as 'sacred' when it gives meaning to the origins of a community, a religion, a nation or a civilisation.

- A story becomes a myth when its **meaning** goes beyond the facts it relates. For example, the myth of Oedipus, according to which a legendary king murdered his father in order to marry his mother, is used in psychoanalysis in relation to the subliminal attraction felt by some boys for their mother and their jealousy of their father.

  In the same way, the Tell myth does not simply tell the story of a father who obtains revenge: it represents, above all, and in a wider sense, the longing of the Swiss for independence.

- A myth is not only associated with ancient legends – there are also **contemporary myths**. Some of them, propagated by mass media, spread certain values across the world.

  Superman is an example of a contemporary myth (created in 1938); almost everyone knows the general characteristics of the character – even without being a fan of the works in which he appears – and knows that he is the standard-bearer of a triumphal America and of its values, whether one identifies with them or not.

In its limited meaning, culture is perceived by totalitarian regimes as a threat. Göring – or sometimes Goebbels – is credited with saying 'When I hear the word culture, I reach for my pistol.' In fact, the quotation comes from Nazi playwright Hanns Johst's play *Schlageter*, in which the character speaking the words refers to releasing the safety-catch of his Browning pistol.

Culture

Culture not only defines 'noble' activities, such as opera or painting. 'Popular' works, such as comic books, fashion and publicity, also fall under the heading. In fact, culture includes knowledge, beliefs, arts, morals, customs, as well as everything that makes it possible for humans to live in society. In this wider sense, 'culture' is the opposite of 'nature'.

Stereotypes and clichés

- A stereotype, just like a cliché, is generally perceived negatively, for it indicates an erroneous perception, even if widely shared. The main characteristics of a stereotype are that it is **repetitive**, rigid and conventional. For whoever uses it, however, it has the advantage of being understood by all.

  The criteria used to stigmatise certain groups can result in stereotypes that have racist or sexist connotations.

- Since stereotypes are quickly and widely understood, they play an active role in facilitating communication. Mass media regularly make use of stereotypes as a kind of **shorthand**.

  Even if few Frenchmen go around wearing a beret and with a baguette under their arm, a subject drawn this way will be immediately recognised by many people as being 'French'. This stereotype is useful for cartoon artists. Moreover, press illustrations could hardly exist without stereotypes.

To create a link between images and the society that produced them, we must base our analysis on a collection of documents that are called a '**corpus**'. It allows us to demonstrate certain repetitive themes (Helvetia's shield, for example), that are the building blocks of social consciousness and enlighten us on its meaning (Helvetia's shield helps to recognise her but also, as a defensive instrument, reminds us of Swiss armed neutrality).

The corpus from which the three illustrations of Helvetia on pages 26–27 are taken comprises over 150 postcards.

Symbols

- A symbol functions by creating an **analogy** – of a more or less obvious nature – between two elements. A lion, for example, evokes strength; the image of a lion permits a symbolic transfer of its characteristics to the context of whatever is being shown.

  Example: the use of a bull in the logo of the Chicago Bulls basketball team evokes a bull's strength.

- An analogy is not always clear and can lead to a **historical construct** with obscure references. A case in point is the cock, which has become the symbol of France.

  The choice of a cock to symbolise France arises from its Latin name gallus, which is the same as the Latin name for the inhabitants of Roman Gaul.

- Symbols, especially **national symbols**, can have **emotional overtones**. This explains their recurring use for political (and commercial) communication.

Symbols

The Swiss cross

The cross on the national flag is the official symbol of Switzerland. There are strict regulations governing its use but it is nevertheless widely used for economic and political purposes.

Origins of the symbol

- The **white cross on a red ground** was already used prior to the birth of the federal State in 1848: the 'Diet' (Assembly of cantonal representatives) adopted it in 1815 as the seal and flag of the Confederation, which was then only an alliance of cantons. Each cantonal army continued to have its own insignia.

- The adoption of a common **military flag** for the whole of Switzerland dates from **1840** – the idea originated with General Guillaume-Henri Dufour.

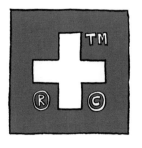

- The Federal Council fixed the precise dimensions of the cross only in 1889: its four branches, equal in length, are one sixth longer than they are wide.

There was an earlier official flag, imposed by the French in 1798, during the short life of the Helvetic Republic: this rectangular standard comprised three horizontal sections in green, red and yellow.

Trade Marks

- The federal law on the protection of official insignia and other public signs, in force since 1932, prohibits use of the Swiss cross as (or as part of) a trade or manufacturer's mark, thus prohibiting, in principle, use of the Swiss cross for publicity purposes. However, there are many **logos** in which it appears, some of them very well known (⋯⫸ p. 24).

The square shape of the Swiss flag comes from its military origins (the only other State with a flag the same shape is the Vatican). When Switzerland joined the United Nations in 2002, the square Swiss flag caused a problem: for reasons of equal treatment between member States, all flags flown in front of the UN headquarters must be rectangular. The Swiss flag was allowed to keep its square shape on condition that its surface area did not exceed that of the others.

- The Swiss cross has acquired major **prominence** for services and manufactured goods. It appears on goods intended both for export and for the internal market. Sometimes, however, it is used on products whose Swissness is limited, e.g. partly manufactured abroad, or with a majority of imported components.

The Swiss origin of a product is normally guaranteed by the Crossbow emblem (⋯⫸ p. 21), but, because of its greater recognition value abroad, the Swiss flag is often used in preference.

A fashionable symbol

- The Swiss cross is in the public domain and – apart from express legal prohibitions – can be used freely, for example for **decorative purposes**.

  A red T-shirt with a white cross is permitted, even if made abroad.

- In 1999, the designer Walter Maurer had the idea of recycling old military blankets into bags, purses and other accessories – a concept already popular since the time when the Freitag brothers, in 1993, made their first bag from the tarpaulin cover of a truck. The Swiss cross with red background on these blankets became the visual highlight of these products.

- The Christmas 2002 edition of the French magazine *Elle* presented a Maurer bag as an essential accessory. The fashion was now launched and several manufacturers – not necessarily Swiss – offer products such as clothes, bags and ceramics that bear the Swiss cross. This gave rise to what some newspapers called **'Swissmania'**.

The Swiss Cross and politics

- The Swiss cross appears on the logos of several **political parties**: CVP, EDU, SVP, the Labour Party (Parti du Travail) and the Democrats. It is also used during **voting campaigns**. In this context, it is supposed to represent all the inalienable values associated with Switzerland.

  The SVP campaigns often use the cross, for example on posters 'against the construction of minarets' (2009), and 'for the expulsion of foreign criminals' (2010). The parties of the left have made more sparing use of the cross: for example, on the occasion of the March 2001 vote 'Yes to Europe' when the Socialist party's poster showed a red European flag, with a white cross in place of one of the 12 stars.

- The Swiss cross, as the official emblem of the country, creates an emphatic reference to Swissness. However, the values that define Switzerland in culture and politics are not cast in concrete. The use of the cross is at the heart of the political process but gives no guarantee that the discourse of the party using it is more Swiss than that of another. On the other hand, it reveals the importance that this party attaches to **national identity**, for the protection of which this party claims to stand as the guarantor.

If the commercial use of the Swiss cross is subject to precise regulation in Switzerland, it is difficult to regulate and control it abroad, especially in countries that do not have close relations with Switzerland. A Belarusian bank was thus able to call itself the BelSwissBank without any fear of sanctions and chose an official seal and logo very closely resembling that of the Swiss Confederation.

Helvetia

Like many countries, Switzerland is represented in allegory by the figure of a woman, an image considered sufficiently neutral that everyone can identify with it.

The best known image of Helvetia is the standing figure displayed since 1874 on 50 centimes, 1 Fr. and 2 Fr. coins – prior to this she was shown seated.

The head in profile on 5, 10 and 20 centimes coins is not that of Helvetia but of *Libertas*, the allegorical figure of Liberty.

Heroine or allegory?

- It is rare for women to acquire national heroic status in Western countries. This role, whether historical or mythical, is normally attributed to men: William Tell, Winkelried in Switzerland, Garibaldi in Italy, William Wallace in Scotland, Alexander Nevsky in Russia, etc.

  France, where Vercingetorix and Joan of Arc share pride of place, is an exception.

- Heroes are often called upon to represent their nation (as in the case of William Tell ⋯⟩ p. 34), but they are not alone; they often have to share this role with **allegorical figures**. Unlike national heroes, these figures will not have accomplished extraordinary deeds at a given historical moment; on the contrary, they are usually represented as timeless and serve as **reference points of national identity**. In Switzerland, that allegorical figure is *Helvetia*.

  In contrast to national heroes, allegorical figures are usually women: Marianne in France, Germania in Germany, Italia turrita in Italy, Hispania in Spain, Britannia in Britain, Columbia in the USA, Mother Svea in Sweden, Mother Russia, Mother Denmark or Mother Norway, for example. John Bull and Uncle Sam are among the rare male allegorical figures.

- Allegorical figures are not generally linked to a story (the story of William Tell is familiar, that of *Helvetia* is not). They are only **symbolic creations** and exist mainly in paintings, statues and various illustrations. Their essential role is to provide a human image of the nation they represent.

  Helvetia 'is' Switzerland, in the same way that a blindfolded woman with a sword and scales in her hands 'is' justice.

- Since Switzerland is a federal State, several allegorical figures have been established at cantonal level. *Berna*, is one example, whose statue stands in front of the western wing of the federal building in Berne; *Geneva* is another, and stands next to *Helvetia* on the national monument at the Mont-Blanc bridge in Geneva.

HELVETIA
STANDING
↓

HELVETIA
SEATED
↓

The stranger we all recognise

- Allegorical figures appeared at the time of the Renaissance (15th and 16th centuries), but it was only in the 19th century that they acquired real importance in national iconography. The first representations of *Helvetia* date from the 17th century, but it was not until the foundation of the federal State in 1848 that she gained prominence and acquired her formal characteristics.

- *Helvetia* is not recognisable from her facial features, which are unremarkable. She is identified by her attributes (even if these vary according to the symbolic aspects that the artist or sponsor wishes to underline).

  - Her most characteristic attribute is her **shield**, which – in addition to making her a defensive figure – is often used to display the federal cross, thus rendering the allegory more easily recognisable;
  - *Helvetia* can also – if not always – hold a **spear** or a sword, or may sometimes be shown with **laurel,** palm or olive branches (symbolising peace).

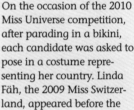

On the occasion of the 2010 Miss Universe competition, after parading in a bikini, each candidate was asked to pose in a costume representing her country. Linda Fäh, the 2009 Miss Switzerland, appeared before the audience dressed as *Helvetia*.

- As a vague incarnation, incorporating whatever values are attributed to her, and rallying the Swiss to the **idea of a nation**, *Helvetia* is the ideal figure for glossing over political, religious and cultural disagreements between the cantons – and her Latin name even permits her to overcome sources of conflict related to language. From the very beginnings of modern Switzerland, *Helvetia* was chosen to decorate coins and stamps.

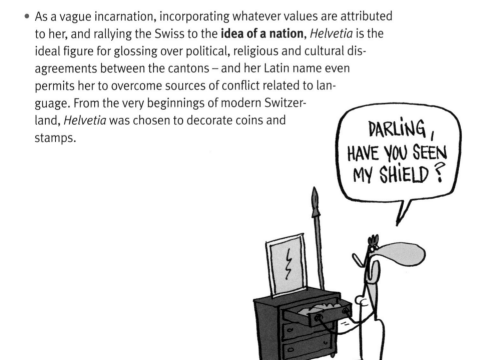

The crossbow

Obviously, the crossbow is linked to the national hero William Tell. However, when it is shown without him, it becomes a separate symbol.

When first used, the crossbow did not enjoy a very good reputation. The fact that it could kill at a distance by piercing armour was considered unchivalrous. Its use by Christians against other Christians was even forbidden by the Lateran Council in 1139, and Pope Innocent II threatened those who made or used it with excommunication.

A little history

• Use of the crossbow spread across Europe from the tenth century onwards. During the Middle Ages, the most famous practitioners of the crossbow were not Swiss but from Genoa. Although some Swiss towns organised militias armed with crossbows in the fourteenth and fifteenth centuries, the pike and halberd were much more characteristic of Swiss soldiers and mercenaries and were generally preferred by them.

• In 1804, Schiller's play re-launched the myth of **William Tell** (····> p. 34) and, with it, the fame of the crossbow. At that time, crossbow shooting became a popular sport in Switzerland.

Swiss crossbowmen were the first to organise themselves in an association and to codify rules for competitions: the Federal Crossbow Association was founded in 1898. Unlike archery, crossbow shooting was never an Olympic discipline.

The crossbow becomes an image

• The oldest graphic representation of a crossbow is on the seal of the Lucerne Town Councillor Johann von Hildisrieden in 1235.

Today, the Municipality of Hildisrieden, in the district of Sursee in the canton of Lucerne, displays a crossbow in its coat of arms. In general, however, the coats of arms of Swiss communes prefer weapons of a more 'noble' character, such as swords.

• As of 1907, the crossbow began to appear on **postage stamps** issued by the Swiss postal service. The aim was to suggest William Tell without actually showing him. The first of these stamps shows a crossbow in the arms of a child whose left hand holds an apple. The crossbow is much bigger than the child, and it thus holds greater potential symbolic meaning.

This series of stamps, in different variations, was in circulation up to the 1930s. A little later, the crossbow re-appeared on stamps, this time alone, in a series celebrating the 1939 National Fair held in Zurich (····> p. 64).

More stamps were issued to commemorate the Swiss origin mark and the anniversaries of its creation.

The Swiss mark of origin

- The **1931** decision to use the crossbow on the **Swiss mark of origin** – initiated by a women's consumer group in Zurich – increased the popularity of the crossbow as an emblem of national identity.

- During this period of economic crisis and re-emphasis on national roots, the aim was to encourage consumption of **Swiss products**. The mark was addressed above all to Swiss consumers and did not aim to promote the sales of Swiss products abroad.

- The choice of the crossbow as a logo for Swiss products was logical: it represented the national hero and was, at the same time, a manufactured product.

This ancestor of the rifle is even more appropriate and effective as a national emblem in a country renowned for the marksmanship of its citizen soldiers (⟶ p. 100).

- In the 1930s and 1940s, the crossbow mark was used in the publicity of Swiss companies which had signed up for the collective mark and it became familiar to everyone in the country. It was stamped, embroidered or printed on the products themselves.

- In the 1960s and 1970s Switzerland enjoyed an upbeat economy and international openness and the Swiss mark of origin lost some of its importance but did not disappear.

- In 1989, the Swiss mark of origin (*Marque Suisse d'Origine* in French; *Schweizerisches Ursprungszeichen* in German; and *Marchio d'Origine Svizzero* in Italian) became **Swiss Label**. English was chosen in preference to the national languages in order to promote Swiss products and services abroad.

Some people were shocked by the use of a foreign language in this context, even more so because it was also used within Switzerland.

Currently, more than 600 companies support *Swiss Label* by paying an annual fee based on their sales volume. For example, for sales below 500,000 Francs, the fee is 180 Francs; a large company with sales of 50 to 100 million Francs, pays a fee of 1200 Francs.

- Today, despite the fact that the number of adherents of *Swiss Label* is increasing, several trademarks give preference to the Swiss cross (⟶ p. 24) because it has greater recognition value for the marketing of Swiss products abroad.

An opinion poll carried out in 2013 on behalf of Swiss Label showed that 82% of Swiss recognised the crossbow symbol.

Edelweiss

Although the Edelweiss is a Swiss national emblem, it is not specific to Switzerland. A plant of Asian origin, it also grows elsewhere and is used as a symbol in other countries.

The German name 'Edelweiss' has replaced the French name 'pied-de-lion', which comes from the botanical appellation *Leontopodium alpinum*. 'Edel' means 'noble' and 'weiss' means 'white'. The name 'edelweiss' has become part of the vocabulary of other languages.

From the Himalayas to Switzerland

- Edelweiss appeared in the Alps after the Quaternary glaciation period (approx. 15,000 years ago). It came from the Himalayas and Siberia, where there are more than 30 wild species. Edelweiss is present throughout the Alps, the Jura, the Pyrenees, the Carpathians and the Apennines. It can also be found in Japan, India and China. There are 41 varieties of Edelweiss in the world.

Botanically speaking, Edelweiss is not 'a' flower but a composite of almost a thousand tiny flowers.

- Edelweiss grows at between 1300 and 3000 metres altitude. During their mountain walks, tourists and hikers used to pick it as a souvenir. This depredation – of a flower that is now famous – led in 1874 to the introduction of protective measures in Germany and Austria, and, in 1879, Switzerland. Nowadays, picking it is either subject to strict protection rules or is simply forbidden.

- The adoption of Edelweiss by the Swiss as a symbol of national identity goes back to the end of the nineteenth century. At that time, the flower was embroidered, carved or painted on many traditional objects as well as on tourist souvenirs. It was also used as a decorative element on chalets and some traditional costumes.

At the beginning of the twentieth century, pressed Edelweiss were attached to postcards, giving them added Alpine authenticity.

A defining logo

In the same way as the Swiss cross, Edelweiss adorn several Swiss products:
- the logo of the **Swiss National Tourist Office** is a Swiss cross in the centre of an Edelweiss flower;
- one of the most widely circulating **women's magazines** in Switzerland is called *Edelweiss* (both French and German editions);
- a Swiss **airline**, set up in 1995 and specialising in charter flights, underlined its Swissness by calling itself 'Edelweiss Air' – names referring to the country itself (Swissair, then Swiss) or to the Swiss cross (Crossair) had already been taken;
- some Swiss **cosmetic products** carry the flower on packaging; it should be noted that, in addition to its role as a national logo, Edelweiss also possess anti-oxidant properties;
- in the **Swiss army**, from brigadier upwards, a stylised Edelweiss flower with a cross in the centre corresponds to the star used in other countries to indicate officer rank.

Edelweiss abroad

- Because Edelweiss grow in many other mountain ranges, the flower is used as a symbol in other countries.

- In 1907, the Austrian emperor Franz-Joseph chose Edelweiss as insignia for his alpine troops. During the first World War, the Austrians gave their emblem to the German alpine troops that came as reinforcements on the Italian front. The emblem was subsequently adopted officially by Nazi Germany. Today, the alpine troops of both Austria and Germany wear it.

  In Austria, an Edelweiss flower is also shown on the two cent Euro coin.

- Edelweiss were, supposedly, Adolf Hitler's favourite flowers (Hitler was born and spent his early life in Austria); hence the name adopted by a small clandestine Nazi group, the 'Edelweiss Pirates', which was active from the fall of the Reich until 1948.

  The same name was used by a group of young Nazi opponents.

- Edelweiss appear on the emblem of the *Südtiroler Volkspartei*, a German-speaking political party in South Tyrol, a region of Italy that was Austrian until 1918. *Stella Alpina* (Italian for 'Edelweiss') is also the name of a regionalist party in the Aosta valley.

Edelweiss are cultivated in Switzerland for use in the cosmetics and agro-food businesses. Recently, *Agroscope*, the Swiss Federal agriculture, food and environmental research organization, created a new variety, with a longer stalk, for sale by florists.

The Swiss cross (currently used logos)

Swiss law does not allow use of the Swiss cross for commercial purposes. However, the symbol is so effective that, despite this prohibition, it is often used as a trademark, with slight changes in proportions that still permit recognition of the national flag.

↑ **The Swiss cross** (postcard, 1941)

The title of this postcard is *History of the Swiss Flag*. This patriotic text, summarised in a few dates, appears on the back of the card.

1289: The men of Schwyz at the siege of Besançon; **1477**: Expeditionary corps at Nancy; **1515**: Retreat from Marignan; **1721–1792**: Diesbach regiment in the service of France; **1798**: Bernese resistance to French invasion; **1862**: Federal army ceremonial flag of 1841; **1871**: Swiss army at Verrières; **1914**: General mobilisation, ceremonial flag of 1890; **1941**: Handing over the flag to an artillery group.

← **The Swiss cross** (handbag, 1999)

This handbag made by the Valais company *Karlen* was made from a military blanket. It was produced in 1999 by the designer Walter Maurer and started a growing fashion for decoration of objects and clothes with the Swiss cross.

Rings im grossen Völkerringen,
Steht sie wie ein Fels im Meer,
Wohlthaten thut sie ihnen bringen,
Und mehret so die Schweizerehr.

Au milieu de l'Europe où la guerre fait rage,
Notre Suisse est debout.-Fidèle à son passé.
Elle reste la main qui soutient et soulage,
Les bras qui sont ouverts à tous, tous les blessés
De cette Europe en sang où la guerre fait rage.

↑ **Helvetia** (postcard, early 20th century)

Helvetia is enthroned in her natural element, Swiss alpine scenery. Edelweiss are doubly present: as part of the landscape and as a symbol on her shield.

← **Helvetia** (postcard, 1916)

Helvetia, here shown in the midst of a Europe at war, is watching over Switzerland (parts of which can be seen) as well as over its frontiers, symbolised by the stone marker. It should be noted that she is wearing armour and a helmet, a rare accoutrement.

→ **Helvetia** (postcard, 1915)

Helvetia, in a humanitarian role, symbolises here the values of the Red Cross. As a result, she dispenses with the warlike attributes shown in the other two images, which makes her less recognisable. In addition the artist felt it necessary to show her name on her crown, but does not specifically identify Marianne, albeit a foreign allegorical figure, since we recognise her easily from her Phrygian bonnet.

↑ **Crossbow** (advertisement, 1937)

When this advertisement was published, the symbol of the crossbow, already in use for several years, was not well enough known that advertising agencies could dispense with a short explanatory text.

←↙ **Crossbow** (stamps, 1909 and 1939)

The crossbow was used regularly on Swiss stamps, either as an emblem of the country or ...

↗↘ **Crossbow** (stamps, 1958 and 1981)

to commemorate the Swiss mark of origin.

**FÊTE NATIONALE 1953
POUR LES SUISSES
À L'ÉTRANGER**

← **Edelweiss** (poster, 1953)

Since 1909, the Swiss committee for the National Day – now known as *Pro Patria* – has organised 1st of August fundraising campaigns for Swiss charitable associations in the cultural and social fields. Commencing with postcards (very popular at the time), the campaigns later included postage stamps with a surcharge and commemorative pins. This poster makes clear that the funds collected will be used for Swiss people abroad – an Edelweiss flower is used as a federating national symbol.

→ **Edelweiss** (poster, 1940s)

Here an Edelweiss flower is used for commercial purposes to promote a brand of cigarettes. This association – that may appear somewhat surprising today – may be justified by the fact that the product is Swiss, since Mahalla cigarettes were made in Richterswil, in the canton of Zurich.

Personalities

Ancestors

Although the lake dwellers and Helvetians really existed, what we think we know about them today is in large part imaginary. The desire to cling to certain myths and other imaginary constructs is stronger than the sometimes more mundane findings of historical research.

Lake people

- Chronologically, the lake peoples' civilisation preceded that of the Helvetians, but the myth associated with them is of more recent date. Thanks to Roman authors, in particular Caesar, the Helvetians have been known for a long time; our knowledge of the lake people, on the other hand, comes from archaeology, a relatively modern branch of science.

- The **myth** of the lake people arose in 1854, when the level of Swiss lakes was very low: the inhabitants of Obermeilen, on the banks of Lake Zurich, took the opportunity to build dams for land reclamation. During the works, a network of poles implanted in the mud was discovered – excavation revealed a large quantity of utensils made of stone, bone and pottery.

- Similar sites were discovered in the lakes of Neuchatel, Bienne, Zug and Constance, as well as others on Lake Zurich. The oldest traces of dwellings were dated to **4000 years BC**.

  Archaeological excavations led to similar discoveries in neighbouring countries, but Switzerland is particularly rich in lake dwelling sites.

- The presence of numerous **stilt supports** on these lake sites led to the conclusion that the dwellings were built in the water. A romantic image of a peaceful and prosperous community, living on platforms in the middle of lakes gained credence. During the second half of the 19th century, this vision, which is no more than an **allegory of an ideal Switzerland**, was reinforced by all kinds of images – artistic and popular – and by clever reconstructions put together for museums and schoolbooks.

- Today, this perception is definitively rejected by scientists. In fact, lake dwellings were most often built on dry land, or, at most, on marshy ground; the stilts were intended to protect them from rises in water level (which, at the time, the inhabitants were unable to forecast) and from humidity near the lakeside.

The Helvetians

- The notion that the Helvetians were the original population of Switzerland appeared in the 15th century. However, as in the case of the lake dwellers, it was in the 19th century that a firm national mythology arose of the Helvetians as the **'official' ancestors** of all the Swiss.

  This role was attributed to them over the claims of the Burgundians, the Lombards, the Raetii, the Alemanii and other tribes that occupied Switzerland in the early ages.

- The Helvetians were chosen to represent the nascent nation, and they even gave their name to the Confederation.

- Some descriptions of the Helvetians in ancient texts certainly reinforced the notion that this tribe should be identified with the modern Swiss. In 100 BC, the Greek philosopher Posidonius described them as 'rich in gold but peaceful'. Julius Caesar, in his *Gallic Wars* (approx. 52 BC), stated that the Helvetians 'exceed the other Gauls in bravery'. These two characteristics found a sympathetic echo among 19th century Swiss in search of identity.

The *Tigurini* were one of the sub-groups of the Helvetians. Their chief, **Divico**, inflicted a bloody defeat on the Roman legions of Consul Lucius Cassius in 107 BC. In the 19th century it was believed that this episode took place on the banks of Lac Léman – it actually took place near the town of Agen in south-west France.

Divico could have played the role of national symbol: contrary to William Tell (⟶ p. 34), his existence is historically authenticated. The legendary hero, however, won out over the historical hero. The Roman humiliation at the hands of the Helvetians nevertheless inspired 19th century patriotic iconography. The painting by Charles Gleyre (⟶ p. 43) is a good example.

Homo Alpinus Helveticus

- During the inter-war years, thinking on the subject of Swiss ancestors was affected by racial considerations. Some people were persuaded by the idea of a **Swiss race**, based on the notion of the *Homo Alpinus Helveticus*, whose portrait was drawn by several anthropologists.

- Between 1927 and 1932, Otto Schlaginhaufen of Zurich studied the morphology of 35,000 recruits, using as his reference some very fanciful characteristics of this supposed ancestor. Although he claimed that his interest was patriotic, he actually sought to demonstrate a certain Swiss 'racial purity'. The result was, however, very disappointing for him: only 1.41% of the sample of young Swiss men matched his **idealised ancestor**.

William Tell

William Tell is the Swiss national hero par excellence. Even though no one really believes any more that he actually existed, his myth is unassailable.

Contrary to popular perception, the person shown on the 5 Franc coin (introduced in 1923 and still in use) is not William Tell but a shepherd. The confusion comes from his hood, which makes him look like the statue of Tell in Altdorf.

The national hero was shown on the 5 Franc note issued in 1914, and on the 100 Franc note issued in 1918.

The legend

On 18 November 1307, William Tell was crossing the main square of the town of Altdorf and deliberately ignored the hat which **Gessler**, the representative of the Habsburgs, had placed on a pole, requiring the inhabitants to pay it obeisance. To punish him, Gessler challenged Tell to shoot with his **crossbow** at an **apple** on the head of his son Walter. Tell succeeded. When Gessler asked why he had kept the second crossbow bolt, Tell replied that, if he had missed the apple, he would have killed him. Gessler sent him to prison. On the way there, he escaped and, in revenge, laid an ambush for Gessler and killed him.

The history of the myth

- The first written mention of William Tell dates from the 15th century. Aegidius Tschudi, a historian from Glarus, subsequently wrote about the episode in his *Chronicon Helveticum* in about 1550. The manuscript was not, however, printed until 1734 when it met with greater interest and made fertile ground for the legend.

- In the first half of the 20th century, some historians considered the legend to be true, particularly in the context of national spiritual defence, a policy launched in the late 1930s to uphold Swiss values and symbols at a time of challenge from fascism and communism.

- Today, there are no historians who give credit to the legend, which is now perceived as a **founding myth**.

Tell or Toko

In Denmark, there is a strikingly similar legend to the Tell myth. The hero, called Toko, confronts King Harald II. There is also an apple on the head of his son, a crossbow and the second bolt, but the end is different: Toko cleverly escapes on his skis.

In 1760, Uriel Freudenberger and Gottlieb Emanuel von Haller anonymously published a book entitled William Tell – a Danish folk tale. *This work, which was considered unpatriotic, was attacked by intellectuals and was even burned in the main square of Altdorf, on the spot where Tell was reputed to have shot at the apple.*

The legend is taken up abroad

As an opponent of tyranny, William Tell was put to use by Enlightenment philosophers and by revolutionaries:
– he enjoyed a high reputation at the time of the American War
  of Independence (1775–1783);
– during the French Revolution, his bust had a place
  of honour in the premises of the Jacobin Club
  (a political club of which Robespierre was a member)
  and a ship of the French fleet bore his name;
– Mikhail Bakounin (1814–1876), the Russian anarchist,
  spoke of Tell as a 'hero of political assassination';
– In 1969, the Palestinian extremists who fired at
  an Israeli aircraft at Zurich airport compared
  themselves to William Tell.

Places of Remembrance

• Three chapels are devoted to the cult of William Tell: in Bürglen, his
  native village; on the Hohle Gasse, where he is supposed to have
  killed Gessler; and at Sissikon, on the banks of Lake Lucerne. The
  latter is the best known.

• The most famous monument dedicated to Tell is the statue erected in
  Altdorf in 1895 (⋯⋗ p. 44). Tell is shown wearing a peasant's hood
  rather than the (less Swiss) plumed hat with which he is portrayed on
  the statue in Lausanne funded by a French donor (also erected in
  1895).

*Ferdinand Hodler's famous 1897 painting shows a Tell very similar to the Altdorf
statue. In it, he is wearing a hood, as does the statue in Montevideo erected by the
Swiss in 1931.*

Tell on stage and screen

Several plays are devoted to Tell. **Schiller**'s version, written in 1804,
confirmed Tell as an international celebrity. Twenty-five years later, the
Italian composer **Rossini** wrote his opera *Guglielmo Tell*, which was
also a great success. From 1900, films took over and Tell is the subject
of more than thirty screen adaptations, produced in many different
countries, as well as a number of television series.

*A popular production about William Tell has been performed regularly in Altdorf since
1899 and, since 1912, in Interlaken.*

Adolf Hitler, fascinated
by William Tell, used a
quotation attributed to him
as a chapter heading in
Mein Kampf: 'The strong man
is mightiest when alone.' In
1941, however, he decided to
prohibit performances of
Schiller's play: as an
apologia for political assassination it might have encouraged such action.

Winkelried

Like William Tell, Winkelried is a legendary figure. Less known abroad, his exemplary self-sacrifice nevertheless gives him an important place among the foundational heroes of Switzerland.

Every year, the victory at Sempach is commemorated on the battlefield with a procession of schoolchildren, musicians and soldiers with uniforms and arms of the period.

The battle of Sempach

• On 9 July 1386, in Sempach in the canton of Lucerne, **Habsburg** troops under the command of Duke Leopold III were attacked by soldiers from Lucerne, reinforced by confederate allies from Uri, Schwyz, Obwald and Nidwald.

• The Habsburgs, in greater numbers, took position on a hill and formed a defensive line of extended lances. The Swiss attacked and managed to break the defence, winning the battle and killing 1800 of the 4000 troops ranged against them, including Leopold III and several knights of his suite.

• Word of this battle spread widely and the Swiss infantry gained the reputation of being unbeatable.

The legend of Winkelried

• The first written source of the legend of Winkelried did not appear until 150 years after the battle of Sempach. According to this version, the Swiss soldiers, struggling to break through the defensive **line of lances,** were given providential assistance by a soldier from Nidwald who threw himself forward and offered a target for the enemy lances. His act proved fatal but allowed the other Swiss to break through the Habsburg ranks and win the battle.

• Before undertaking his heroic act, Winkelried is supposed to have said to his fellow soldiers: 'I will open a breach for you – **take care of my wife and children.**'

• There is no historical evidence to confirm this act of bravery. Moreover, it is unlikely that the action of a single soldier could have turned the tide of such a battle. In essence, the story has symbolic significance and personalises, in Winkelried, the determination of the Swiss when faced with a more powerful enemy.

Even if there is no doubt about the legendary character of the Winkelried story, his name is almost always mentioned in historical accounts of the battle of Sempach. Moreover, until recently, the vast majority of schoolbooks gave him implicit historical credibility.

The Winkelried cult

- Winkelried is the **number 2 Swiss hero**. Although his legend relates to a battle that actually happened and thus has a stronger historical basis, William Tell retains his top ranking in Swiss hearts.

- Tell was acting essentially for revenge, but the story of Winkelried allows a more collective construct: the man from Nidwald was deliberately sacrificing himself for the general good.

The federal Winkelried Foundation was created in 1886 to provide assistance to military personnel wounded in the course of duty or to their families in case of death. In 1995, coverage was extended to personnel involved in peace-keeping duties.

In the collective memory

- Winkelried gave his name to the second steamer launched on Lac Léman in 1824. At this time, these boats represented the cutting edge of technology, which put them into the public spotlight. The *Winkelried* had a capacity of 300 passengers, 100 more than the first steamer on the lake, the *William Tell*.

  The Winkelried *was operated by a company in Geneva, a canton that only joined the Confederation in 1815. The choice of one of the heroes of early Switzerland for the steamer's name thus has great symbolic significance, as Geneva was then considered 'the most French of Swiss cities.' In 1870, the jewel of the Geneva fleet, the largest and fastest on the lake at that time, was baptised* Winkelried II.

- There is a monument to Winkelried in Stans, capital of the canton of Nidwald. It was made in Rome in 1865 by Ferdinand Schlöth, using Carrara marble, and was brought to Switzerland by various means of transport, including a specially made railway waggon.

- In Sempach there is a granite slab bearing the words 'Here, in 1386, Winkelried opened a breach for his companions.' Several paintings celebrate the hero, of which the best known is by Konrad Grob: *Winkelried at Sempach* (⤑ p. 45).

Heidi

It sometimes happens that a single character can represent a whole country. Such a person can be historical (e.g. General Guisan), allegorical (Helvetia) or, less frequently, fictional. In Switzerland, Heidi fulfils that role.

The old school building in the town of Hirzel in the canton of Zurich, where Johanna Spyri learned to read and write, has been made into a museum. A large part of the exhibition is devoted to Heidi.

The novels

- From 1871, Johanna Spyri published a series of children's books. The first novel with Heidi as heroine – *Heidis Lehr- und Wanderjahre* (Heidi's years of learning and travel) – was published in **1880**.

  It was followed a year later by Heidi kann brauchen, was es gelernt hat *(Heidi begins to use what she has learned) – the two novels were published in a single volume as* Heidi *in English.*

- It was a great success and many translations rapidly followed. Today, *Heidi* is one of the most widely translated books in the world.

  Charles Tritten, who took great liberties with the original text in his French translation, decided to write sequels to Johanna Spyri's work. Beginning in 1934, he wrote novels in which Heidi is the main character, including (English titles) Heidi Grows Up *and* Heidi's Children.

Cinema and Television

- Some twenty films were inspired by Heidi's adventures:
  - from 1920, **film** producers in the US took up the story, already familiar to audiences there;
  - in 1937, the child star Shirley Temple played the role and boosted the fame of the girl from the Swiss alps;
  - the first **TV series** (English) dates from 1953.

    Many other productions – American, German and Franco-Swiss – followed.

ON YOUR LEFT, THE PASTURE WHERE HEIDI'S GOAT ONCE GRAZED!

HEIDI TOURS

- A further success was registered in 1974, when the Japanese producer Isao Takahata brought out an **animated film** series called *Heidi, Girl of the Alps*. Its 52 episodes are still being shown on TV.

  Other media contributed to the publicising of the image of Heidi throughout the world: several illustrated children's books were published, some accompanied by an audio recording; records were made with the sound track of the animated film series or TV films; a comic book was published; and, in 2004, there was even a musical comedy produced in Walenstadt in the canton of St. Gallen, entitled Heidi – the Musical.

Advertising imagery

- Heidi has been represented with various facial features – with brown or blond hair, short or long – and her story has been adapted to various periods. Markus Imboden's 2001 Swiss film, for example, places her in a contemporary context. Despite this, it is fairly easy to recognise her:
  - she is generally accompanied by a **goat**;
  - most often she is shown barefoot;
  - she appears in a **mountain** environment.

'Heidi' is the diminutive form of the first name of Johanna Spyri's character. Her actual name was 'Adelheid' (corresponding to 'Adelaide' in English).

- Having become a Swiss icon, Heidi earned the right to appear on Swiss stamps (in 1951 and 2010) and on a commemorative coin (in 2001, for the 100th anniversary of Johanna Spyri's death).

  In 2001, she even appeared on a German postage stamp.

- Since it evoked both Switzerland and its mountainous natural environment, the name 'Heidi' was used by *Migros* for its range of Swiss-made 'alpine' products.

  The labels on these products are decorated with pictures of Heidi in different décors, using a style reminiscent of the pictures in the children's books.

- In the area of fashion and design, the company *heidi.com* markets clothes intended to recall, in the urban environment of the 21st century, the positive characteristics of the famous Heidi from the Alps.

  The logo of this company reflects the 'manga' character of the animated film (····} p. 46).

HEIDI LTD.
FACTORY FOR
NATURAL PRODUCTS

Heidi and Swiss identity

- Heidi's international success results in her being used as a representative of Switzerland abroad. Some tourist visitors to Switzerland expect to find part of the universe inhabited by their heroine. But her adventures and the places in which she lived belong to a Switzerland of myth, of mountain and peasant people, far from the rapidly industrialising country that Switzerland had become at the end of the 19th century.

- The quest for the picturesque, frequently the aim of bus-loads of tourists, can, however, be satisfied by the faithful re-creation of places that embody the spirit of Johanna Spyri's novels.

  In 1997, the region of Walenstadt in the canton of St. Gallen proclaimed itself 'Heidiland'; and, in 1998, the little town of Maienfeld (canton of Graubunden) transformed a group of houses into a 'Heidi village', where one can see her goats and visit her grandfather's chalet. Thanks to this initiative, Maienfeld receives 50,000 tourists annually, half of them from Japan.

General Guisan

General Guisan symbolised the 'spirit of resistance' at the time of the 1939–1945 general mobilisation, and enjoyed unanimous support in Switzerland. He was from the French-speaking part of the country but spoke fluent Swiss German and knew how to speak to the people, many of whom created a cult in his name that lasted long after the end of the war.

A career soldier

- Henri Guisan was born on 21 October 1874 in Mézières (canton of Vaud). He joined the artillery and was promoted to Lieutenant in 1894. A professional soldier, Guisan – then with the rank of Lieutenant General – was appointed General by the Federal Assembly on **30 August 1939** by 204 of 231 votes; he was **65 years** old.

- A central figure in the **mobilisation**, General Guisan was praised by all regions of Switzerland. On 12 April 1960, 300,000 people attended his funeral in Lausanne.

General Wille, on the other hand, in office during the first World War, was far from obtaining unanimous support. He was particularly criticised for his pro-German attitude.

IT'S TIME FOR A GENERAL MOBILISATION...

...OF ALL THE MEDIA!

A good communicator

- It is difficult to assess Guisan's strategic abilities, since they were never tested in battle. He was, however, a proven master of communication with the public.

- Guisan was very particular about his image, accepting speaking engagements on various occasions, and cultivated his presence in the media. A large part of the national **propaganda** of the period was based on his charisma and he became the focus of greater attention than the Federal Council.

The General's public image was kept carefully under control: between 1939 and 1945, 5600 photos of him were banned from publication.

- Several of his actions were purely **symbolic** in character: the 'Rütli Report', bringing together 400 senior officers on the mythical meadow (····≯ p. 80); or the so-called 'Promotion des Rangiers', a ceremony on a frontier pass ('Col des Rangiers' in the Jura mountains) celebrating, in front of a statue of a sentinel, the mobilisation of the 1st World War. These events were mainly for the media and had very little strategic significance.

The strategy of the 'national redoubt' (····≯ p. 68), promoted by Guisan, was also largely symbolic: it reflected the spirit of resistance by taking it into the heart of the Alps, symbol of the country itself.

In Switzerland, generals are only appointed in time of war. There have so far been four: Guillaume-Henri Dufour (Sonderbund War, 1847), Hans Herzog (Franco-Prussian War 1870–1871); Ulrich Wille (1st World War 1914–1918); and Henri Guisan (2nd World War 1939–1945).

Some dark spots

- The idealised image of the General was tarnished a little in the 1980s. Some critical historians, as well as film-makers – such as Frank Pichard in his 1985 film *Quelques retouches au portrait du Général Guisan (Some retouching of General Guisan's portrait)* – drew attention to some dark spots in Guisan's character.

- His admiration for Pétain and Mussolini is a problem, as is his secret meeting in March 1943 with Walter Schellenberg, right-hand man of Heinrich Himmler, head of the SS. Moreover, a letter from Guisan dated January 1941 expressed concern about the involvement of Jews in military film-making.

The following is an extract from this letter (translation): 'I am in possession of credible information suggesting that the presence of foreign personalities and organisations in Swiss film-making is dangerous. Is it correct that a Jew called Gross-feld, naturalised and of German origin, who is a member of the Association of Swiss Film-makers, participates in the work of the film-making committee of the army? Is it correct that two other Jews, Rothschild and Zikendraht, belong to the army film-making service? In the personnel employed by you, are there other Jews?'

One of the overcoats worn by General Guisan between 1939 and 1945 was sold by the auction house Stuker in Bern in 2011. The asking price of 7000 Francs was substantially outbid and the relic went for 155,000 Francs. One of the General's caps had already been sold in 2006 for more than 100,000 Francs.

Guisan in bronze

- On the general's death in 1960, a fund-raising campaign was started for the purpose of erecting a **monument** to him. The Zurich sculptor, Otto Bänninger, was chosen and the monument was inaugurated in Ouchy, Lausanne, in 1967.

The event received much media attention but there was criticism. For example:
– the statue shows Guisan on horseback wearing an overcoat – this was never the case;
– his posture was considered too rigid and martial for a person close to the people;
– his horse is not very sturdy and resembles a gazelle;
– the monument should have been placed in the centre of Lausanne.

↑ **Ancestors** (photograph, 1882)

These participants in a historical procession in Neuchatel in 1882 are disguised as 'lake dwellers'. They are posing in costumes resonant of archaeological discoveries of the period (tools, in particular) combined with fanciful elements drawn from popular imagery.

←↙ **Ancestors** (trade cards, 1931, 1939)

For a long time, manufacturers of cigarettes, chocolate and soup gave away small collectible prints for publicity purposes (e.g. cigarette cards) with their products. They were very popular between the end of the 19th and the middle of the 20th century; collected by many people, they covered a wide range of subjects. *Liebig*, a manufacturer of food products, began distributing such cards in 1872. Several of the series depicted the theme of the lake people and propagated the fanciful theory that their huts were built on platforms in the middle of lakes, as shown on these two examples from 1931 and 1939.

↑ **Ancestors** (painting, *The Romans passing under the yoke*, 1858)

In the middle of the 19th century, Charles Gleyre, a painter from Vaud living in Paris, was commissioned by the cantonal authorities to produce this painting. It shows the victory of the Helvetian chief, Divico, over the Romans in 107 BC. At the time, it was believed that the battle took place near Villeneuve, but Gleyre shifted the scene nearer to Montreux, which allowed him to show the 'Dents du Midi' in the background, a series of peaks visible from there. In the 20th century, historians proved that the Helvetians fought with the Romans in France, near the town of Agen, some 700 kilometres away. While the painting glorifies the victorious Helvetians, the dignity of the Romans is also emphasised, with their proud facial expression and athletic bodies.

←↙ William Tell (posters, 1950, 2006)

These two posters instrumentalise the design of the Tell statue in Altdorf: a left-wing party and the manufacturer of a sandwich spread both seek to be recognised in the figure of the national hero and to claim his virtues for themselves.

In one case, the crossbow is replaced by a spade and pick – in the other by the outstretched arm of the child on its mother's back, offering the product on a sandwich.

↑ Guillaume Tell (sculpture, 1895)

At the end of the 19th century, a competition was organised for the replacement of the old Tell statue in Altdorf. The project of the sculptor Richard Kissling was chosen, showing Tell as a mountain peasant, in a costume that could still be widely seen in central Switzerland at the time. The hood, a feature of depictions of Tell, dates from that period. Previously, he was shown most frequently with a plumed hat, in the style of Robin Hood. The statue on the Montbenon esplanade in Lausanne shows him in this way – the gift of a French donor, it was finished in the same year as the Altdorf statue (1895).

↑ **Winkelried** (postcard, 1910)

The Swiss fund for the national day (⋯⟶ p. 29) put its first postcard on sale for the celebration of the 1st of August 1910. It cost 20 centimes and shows William Tell and Winkelried as 'guardians of the homeland'. The income from this first fund-raising activity went to the victims of flooding in central Switzerland that year.

↑ **Winkelried** (postcard, early 20th century)

This postcard shows the dead Winkelried (recognisable because of the lances in his body) being honoured by an angel and by his fellow-soldiers. At a price of 20 centimes, the aim of the card was to collect funds for the Winkelried Foundation in aid of wounded soldiers.

→ **Winkelried** (painting, *Death of Winkelried at Sempach*, 1878)

This painting of the battle of Sempach was donated to the Federal Council by the artist, Konrad Grob. It will be noted that one of the warriors is wearing a cow's skull on his head, as in the case of Divico in the painting by Charles Gleyre (⋯⟶ p. 43) and some of the lake dwellers on the photo of the 1882 historical procession (⋯⟶ p. 42). This head-covering, reminiscent of rural virtues, was used recurrently as a Swiss symbol, despite the fact that, in reality, it was very rarely worn.

↑ **Heidi** (poster, 1937)
→ **Heidi** (animated film, 1974)

Heidi, as a fictional character, has been widely publicised around the world. There have been two high points in the development of her popularity, both occurring much later than the death of her creator: the 20th Century Fox film of 1937 (with Shirley Temple), and the 1974 Japanese animated film *Heidi*, produced by Isao Takahata.

↑ **General Guisan** (plate, 1960s)

General Guisan's portrait was so popular that it adorned many souvenirs, as in the case of this plate, which found a place in the china cabinet or on the wall of many Swiss families.

← **General Guisan**
  (Catholic weekly magazine, 1941)

The magazine *L'Echo Illustré* put General Guisan on its front page several times. The occasion chosen for the issue of 27 September 1941 was the honorary citizenship granted to the Commander-in-Chief by the commune of Pully. The photograph reflects his proximity to the people, bending down towards the girl, despite his status as a soldier. Values linked to the land are also emphasised – by means of the traditional peasant costume of Vaud worn by the girl – the general was accompanied by his wife, even if we cannot make out her face. During the war, Guisan was the personality most often portrayed on magazine covers in Switzerland.

Products

Chocolate

Despite the fact that its raw material has nothing Swiss about it, Swiss chocolate enjoys such a high reputation that several foreign manufacturers use pictures of cows, mountains and chalets to sell their chocolate.

It is said that Christopher Columbus was given cocoa beans by the indigenous population, but thought they were goat dung and threw them overboard.

A recent story

- Industrial production of chocolate began in Switzerland in the **first half of the 19th century**. At the beginning of the 20th century, exports of what was formerly a luxury product grew by leaps and bounds, rising from 680 metric tons in 1890 to 3140 in 1900, and 10,756 in 1910.

  The Swiss have the highest consumption of chocolate in the world at 12 kilos per inhabitant in 2013.

- Switzerland's association with chocolate results from the large-scale **industrial production** and export of Swiss chocolate. It required innovation, and the production methods revolutionised the original recipe, with the invention of **milk chocolate** (in 1875) and 'fondant' (in 1879).

- As in the case of many industrial products, the marketing of chocolate makes use of many different images: logos and trademarks, images on packaging, illustrations in publicity etc. These differentiate the product from that of competitors and link it to a tradition that gives it positive positioning.

From the colonies ...

- Chocolate comes from South America. In 17th century Europe it was widely consumed in liquid form as a drink. The start of industrial production of chocolate led to rising demand for cocoa beans: to meet this need, cocoa trees were introduced in Africa in the 19th century.

- It is not, therefore, surprising that **colonial imagery** began to influence the design of the first chocolate wrappings, especially in countries with colonies.

  In France, for example, an African was shown for many years on publicity for the Felix Potin brand. It is also worth noting that, until about the 1920s, images of Africans were associated with products of dark colour, such as coffee or shoe polish.

- Today, images linked to the countries where cocoa is produced are reappearing on 'fair trade' products, harking back in a way to the earlier colonial illustrations.

... to the Alps

- When Swiss chocolate gained in prestige at the end of the 19th century, its manufacturers realised that its attraction could be enhanced – both on the national and international markets – by the use of typically Swiss images. Colonial imagery came to be replaced by **alpine imagery**.

- Milk chocolate gave Swiss production a competitive advantage and manufacturers promoted images linked to milk, a product with local characteristics, rather than to cocoa, an imported product.

- Today, although the description 'Swiss chocolate' is almost always used, the major brand names make less use of Swiss clichés on their packaging. However, the lesser-known manufacturers sometimes feel the commercial need to insist on their origin.

- **Cows, mountains** (often both) and occasionally a **chalet** are the images most often used, even on chocolate not made in Switzerland, demonstrating that the linkage of chocolate with alpine themes is internationally wide-spread.

Toblerone was introduced in 1908 by the Bernese company Tobler & Cie, (today part of the American company Kraft Foods). Its first logo depicted an eagle and was replaced in the 1920s by a Bernese bear. The eagle returned in 1930 and currently, from 2000, the packaging shows the universally recognisable Matterhorn, although if you look carefully you will find a bear in profile still hiding on the mountain.

'Postcard' chocolate

- Some 20% of chocolate sales in Switzerland are linked to tourism. The packaging of 'souvenir chocolate' uses images of typically Swiss locations. Given its reputation, the Matterhorn is frequently mobilised.

- As a symbol of Switzerland, chocolate can easily be partnered with other national symbols and clichés, and not only through the images used on packaging: in souvenir shops and airport 'duty frees' there are chocolate Swiss army knives, bundles of Swiss banknotes and gold bars in chocolate, chocolate cows and even Swiss passports made of chocolate.

In 2008, the Swiss postal service issued a stamp showing a chocolate bar which also had a chocolate scent.

Cheese

The renown of some Swiss cheeses has not served their producers well. Emmental and Gruyère, for example, became generic names associated with products that no longer have any connection with Switzerland.

Several 'Swiss' cheeses are also produced abroad, such as 'Heidi Farm Raclette' made by a company in Tasmania (Australia) that also makes 'Gruyere' and 'Tilsit' – but not Emmental, despite it being the 'Swiss cheese' most produced abroad.

A little history

- It is thought that cheese – in a form similar to curds, frequently with added herbs – has been made in Switzerland since the **earliest recorded history** (in Gruyère and lower Valais).

'Firm' (as opposed to soft) cheese appeared in the 15th century. Because it kept longer, it enlarged the market by making it possible to export Swiss cheeses, most notably to Italy, France and Germany.

- Around 1860, trade in Swiss cheese grew substantially. Prices went up and production – until then mainly in the mountains – also shifted to the plains.

- During the second World War, exports were stopped. The aim was to meet local food needs, not to prevent trade in what was earlier considered to be a product of military value.

'Swiss cheeses are much appreciated throughout Europe not only for their aromatic flavour, but also for the length of time that they can be kept (up to one hundred years), which makes them very appropriate for military and naval use.' (Swiss Library of Trade and Industry, 1840)

- Today, the most exported Swiss cheese variety is **Emmental** (75% of the local production) and the main importing countries are the same as in the 15th century. Within Switzerland, **Gruyère** is the most widely sold Swiss cheese (however, for cheese of all origins, Mozzarella is the champion).

The mountain shepherd ('Armailli')

- The image of Swiss cheese is linked to a few places and people, of whom the most important is the mountain shepherd ('armailli' in French). Originally a master cheese-maker responsible for a small production unit on the mountain pasture, he later found his way down to the valleys as cheese-making became progressively concentrated there in the 19th century.

Their alpine costumes, together with the ceremonial transfer of the herd to its summer mountain pastures and the accompanying songs (e.g. the Ranz des Vaches) remain part of the culture.

- The image of the 'armailli' gained its permanent contours with the idealisation of pastoral life in the literature and painting of the 18th century and then, from the late 19th century, in films and the illustrated press.

The image of the 'armailli' is marked in particular by the traditional costumes of Appenzell, Toggenburg, Emmental and Gruyère, as well as by certain utensils, such as the special rack ('oji') used to bring the cheese down on men's backs.

The holes in Gruyère cheese

- The holes in Gruyère cheese enjoy international celebrity, even if the cheese made in **Switzerland** actually has none. There is indeed a Gruyère with holes, but it is made in **France**. And although the Gruyère region is in Switzerland and the level of production of the Swiss cheese is nine times higher than that of the French equivalent, the association of holes with Gruyère is difficult to eradicate.

The French comedian, Coluche, said: 'Politicians are like the holes in Gruyère – the more Gruyère there is the more holes there are, and, unfortunately, the more holes there are, the less Gruyère there is.' Another comedian, Francis Blanche, commented that 'a day without a practical joke is like a Gruyère without holes.' The French author Jean-Loup Chiflet wondered: 'Once you have eaten the Gruyère, what has become of the holes?' And the English adventurer Peter Fleming, brother of Ian, the creator of James Bond, evokes the holes in Gruyère when describing gaps in a wall in his book Brazilian Adventure.

- The financial issues linked to the appellation Gruyère (and thus the presence or not of holes) are significant and producers in both countries fought legal battles to retain it.

In 2001, France registered 'Gruyère' as a 'certified designation of origin' (Appellation d'origine contrôlée – AOC) for its cheese. In 2007, Switzerland did the same, while France filed a request for a 'protected designation of origin' (Appellation d'origine protégée – AOP) with the European Union. In 2010, following international arbitration, Switzerland obtained the AOP, while France had to be content with the less prestigious label 'Indication géographique protégée – IGP'.

Jet-propelled raclette

- During the 1992–1993 ski season, the sponsor of the Swiss Ski Federation was the Swiss Cheese Union. The **Swiss skiing team** caused a sensation with a yellow ski-suit covered in simulated holes that resembled the texture of Emmental cheese.

- This new uniform drew wide-spread attention, particularly in the press, which wrote of 'racing cheese' or 'jet-propelled raclette'. The suit was perceived as amusing, even cheeky, but it referred to one of the main Swiss products familiar to foreigners, and, at the same time to identity-based values.

In Switzerland, almost half of milk production is used for making one of the 450 varieties of Swiss cheese – made mainly from cow's milk. For every 560 kilograms of cheese made from cow's milk, only 1 kilogram of cheese from goat's or sheep's milk is produced. Moreover, the little goat accompanying Heidi is relatively rare in the country. At the beginning of the 20th century, 420,000 head were counted: in 2005, the number had dropped to 74,000.

Swiss Army knife

Originally, the Swiss Army knife was a simple military folding knife, similar to that used in many other armies. In the course of time, it became a standard-bearer for the country.

The first knife adopted by the Swiss army, known as the '1890 Model', included a blade, a tin-opener, a screwdriver and a small pick (commonly called in English a 'thing for getting stones out of horses' hooves'). At that time, no Swiss company was able to guarantee sufficiently rapid delivery and the army had to turn to the German manufacturer *Wester* in Solingen. More than a century later, the situation was reversed: *Victorinox* has been producing pocket knives for the German army since 2003.

Military origins

- In **1891,** the Swiss army officially adopted a folding pocket knife. In addition to practical applications, such as for meals, it was also intended for dismantling a rifle.

  It looked different from the red knife with a white cross that is well-known today: it was big, strong and fairly heavy. The handle was made of darkened wood and was not decorated with the cross.

- In 1897, a certain Karl Elsener began non-military sales of a 'Swiss officer's and sports knife'. It was different from the official army model in that it included a corkscrew, and, from 1909, was decorated with the Swiss cross.

  In 1909, Karl Elsener called his company 'Victoria', after his mother's name. In 1921, the use of stainless steel for making blades ('acier inoxydable' in French) led him to choose the trade name 'Victorinox'. In 2005, his company bought out its competitor Wenger while retaining its trade mark. These are the only trade names that can be used for 'genuine' Swiss Army knives.

- Shortly after the end of the second World War, many American soldiers stationed in neighbouring countries visited Switzerland, which had been spared from hostilities. Each one received 150 Francs from the US government as pocket money, which was a boon for the tourist business. Among the items brought back by the **GIs** from their Swiss tour was the Swiss officer's knife, more attractive than the soldier's version, that was sold freely in the shops. This was the start of the international reputation of the **Swiss Army knife**.

A synonym for multi-functional

- The Swiss Army knife spread rapidly around the world and – immediately associated with Switzerland – became a standard-bearer for the country. Its image evokes also multi-functional applications and high performance in miniature. Moreover, both in advertising and day-to-day parlance, the term 'Swiss Army knife' is used today in this sense.

  For example: The multi-functional Mistral *class helicopter carrier of the French navy is nicknamed 'the floating Swiss Army knife'; publicity for the computer programme* Perlan, *which enhances the performance of a well-known video player, refers to it as 'a Swiss army knife for* QuickTime'.

A medium for an image

- The Swiss Army knife is an important national symbol, so much so that in 2009–2010 the national museum in Prangins devoted an exhibition to it. It also conveys other symbols of Switzerland: the Swiss cross on the handle and the crossbow stamped on the blade, which guarantees that it is made in Switzerland (⋯⋯> p. 21).

- The handle can also be decorated with logos (several companies offer personalised versions to their clients), with symbols of identity such as an Edelweiss, or with tourist locations, which emphasise the knife's role as a **souvenir item**.

Considered a tool and not a weapon, the Swiss Army knife travelled freely in the pocket of its owner, even on airlines. However, following the events of 11 September 2001, stricter rules were introduced prohibiting it from being carried on board, thus having a negative effect on sales at airport shops. According to Victorinox, this resulted in a 20% drop in sales.

In 2013, the US authorities made a concession by allowing passengers to board with knives with blades of less than 6cm in length and 1cm in width.

A star

- The Swiss Army knife has gained prominence as the perfect survival tool in several works of fiction. One of its most active promoters is certainly the TV series *MacGyver* (shown from 1985 to 1992); the eponymous hero, renowned for his ability to get out of all kinds of situations, used the Swiss Army knife as his favourite tool.

The Danny Boyle film 127 Hours (screened in 2001) tells the story of a man trapped under a boulder and forced to amputate his arm with a pocket knife in order to escape. The film critic of the Swiss French-language newspaper Le Temps described the film as a 90-minute commercial for Swiss knives.

A work of art?

- In 1977, the famous New York Museum of Modern Art (MoMA) acquired the Victorinox model *Swiss Champ* to add to its collections in the category 'Architecture and Design'.

Other art museums, including Munich's State Museum of Applied Art, followed the trend.

- In 1985, at the Venice film festival, an enormous Swiss Army knife, made by the Swede Claes Oldenburg, was placed alongside the Arsenal Canal.

- In 1998, the artist Thomas Hirschhorn questioned his relationship to Switzerland in an exhibition at the Bern art museum under the title *Swiss Army Knife*.

Fondue, Rösti and Raclette

Switzerland may not be renowned for its cuisine, but it has several specialities; some are typical of a region (e.g. 'Papet Vaudois', a hotpot of leek and potatoes – or 'Zürcher Geschnetzeltes', strips of veal cooked with mushrooms and cream); only a few have acquired national identity.

Fondue

- The origin of fondue has not been clearly established, but it is very old and several regions claim paternity. It seems, however, to be a dish originating in French-speaking rather than German-speaking Switzerland, even if today it has acquired the status of a **Swiss national dish**.

- The first written recipes for fondue are relatively recent. For example, a cookbook of 1885 from the Zurich housekeeping school suggests one, even though it seems today a little unorthodox. The spread of the present recipe (cheese melted in white wine, with added garlic and corn starch) only goes back to the beginning of the 20th century.

- In the 1930s, cheese producers were faced with overproduction and adopted fondue as a new sales opportunity. It became a mass product in the **1960s** thanks to pre-prepared packages.

I THINK I DROPPED–

OFF WITH YOUR CLOTHES!

There are several fondue recipes that vary according to region. Fondue with 100% 'vacherin fribourgeois' (a semi-soft cheese made with milk from cows of the Fribourg breed) is eaten lukewarm. There are other varieties, for example with tomato or 'bolets' (porcini mushrooms), and even chocolate (this recipe does not contain cheese!).

Fondue and fiction

- Sometimes, a person who loses a piece of bread in the fondue has to perform a forfeit, which might include kissing another guest.

- In the 1978 film *The Swissmakers* (directed by Rolf Lyssy), the correct preparation of fondue is a crucial test for obtaining Swiss nationality. The 1979 French cult film *Les Bronzés font du ski* (directed by Patrice Leconte) also celebrates fondue, even if it is actually eaten in the Savoy Alps in France.

Fondue was presented at the New York World Fair in 1940. It was fashionable in the 1970s and then its popularity declined. To re-launch it, Swiss producers offered tastings in the streets of New York in 2007 – but were careful to Americanise it by serving it in hot dog buns.

Rösti

- The date at which the first Rösti was prepared is not known, but the basic product, potatoes, was not grown in Switzerland until the beginning of the 17th century. A dish of **Bernese origin**, Rösti gradually conquered German-speaking Switzerland and then the rest of the country (where it remains less popular).

- Rösti gave rise to the name **Röstigraben** (German), or **Barrière de Rösti** (French), to define the cultural frontier between German-speaking and French-speaking Switzerland.

This 'barrier' was in evidence at the time of the 1st World War, when Western Switzerland favoured France and her allies, and the German-speakers supported Germany and the Central Powers. But no one then spoke of the Röstigraben. The expression became more popular in the press during the 1970s to illustrate the division of Swiss opinion in the debate on the creation of the Jura canton.

Raclette

- The origins of raclette probably go back to the Middle Ages in the **Pennine Alps of Valais**, although similar ways of preparing cheese exist in other countries.

- Formerly, as evidenced in some 16th century archives, raclette was known simply as 'roasted cheese'. The first author to use the term 'raclette' was the historian Eugène Rambert in his 1874 work *Les Alpes suisses*.

An article on Valais appearing in the Journal de Genève of 21 December 1887 contained the word 'raclette', but the author felt it necessary to include a description: 'Local custom requires that raclette (full-fat cheese roasted on embers) be served in this situation.'

- The word 'raclette' became widely used during the 20th century, especially after the Cantonal Fair in Sion in 1909, when the dish was declared 'a national Valais delicacy'.

- Raclette cheeses are produced in a number of countries: France is the number one producer with 50,000 metric tons per year. In 2003, however, only Valais raclette obtained the **AOC** ('certified designation of origin') label.

Of the 12,000 metric tons of raclette cheese produced annually in Switzerland, only 2000 tons come from Valais.

Since 1994, Swiss industrial activity linked to raclette consumption has spent almost 2 million francs annually on marketing, resulting in a short space of time in an increase of 52% in sales.

Typical brands

Some commercial brands are firmly identified with Switzerland; sometimes because they 'represent' the country abroad (Ovaltine/Ovomaltine and Ricola) and sometimes because they are almost exclusively marketed in Switzerland (Cenovis, Migros, Le Parfait, Rivella).

Cenovis

This sandwich spread was developed in Rheinfelden (canton of Aargau) in 1931, using surplus yeast from breweries. In 1955, because it was considered a valuable nutritional supplement, Cenovis was added to the Swiss army's survival rations, thus increasing its popularity. At the end of the 20th century there was a drop in sales and the product was taken over by a Geneva financier who re-launched it with a publicity campaign that made abundant reference to symbols of Swiss national identity (⋯⟩ p. 44).

Despite its Swiss-German origin, Cenovis is better known today in Western Switzerland; a 2009 study by the market research agency Isopublic showed that it has 75% recognition among French-speakers in Switzerland and only 28% among German-speakers.

Migros

- Founded in 1925, Migros is the main retail chain in Switzerland. It has 37% of the market for food products, compared to the Coop with 35%. Its founder, Gottlieb Duttweiler, lowered prices by working without middlemen and selling his basic food products in simple packaging.

  At the beginning, customers were served by mobile shops that travelled from village to village. For a long time, Migros only sold products under its own label.

- During the inter-war period, the company was perceived as such a threat to small businesses that it was banned from some cantons. In 1935, Duttweiler allied himself with the Independent party *(Landesring der Unabhängigen/Alliance des Indépendants)*, which came to the defence of his concept.

- Duttweiler believed in 'socially oriented capital'. The allocation of 1% of company turnover to cultural projects is the legacy of this philosophy, as is the absence of alcohol and tobacco from its shelves.

  In 2007, Migros acquired 70% of the shares of the retailer Denner, one of the leaders in sales of alcohol and tobacco in Switzerland.

In 1954, Gottlieb Duttweiler set up Migros Türk, a Turkish company still in business and using an almost identical logo to that of its big sister; since 1975, however, it no longer has any affiliation with Migros.

- Although there are Migros stores throughout Switzerland, and generations of Swiss consumers have grown up with its products and philosophy, it does not have much of a presence abroad.

  Some words linked to the company have become part of day-to-day language, e.g. 'Migros data' (a system indicating 'sell-by' dates launched in 1967, long before its competitors). A 2010 study by GfK Business Reflector showed that Migros is the best known trade name in Switzerland.

Ovaltine/Ovomaltine

A soluble powder with a barley malt base, containing eggs and milk, *Ovomaltine* was created in 1904 by the pharmacist Albert Wander. Export sales began in 1906, especially to Great Britain and Italy where it was very successful.

The British market – where it is called 'Ovaltine' – is the biggest in Europe.

Even though it has been owned since 2002 by a British multinational, its Swiss origin is still part of its trade identity.

Le Parfait

Le Parfait – the first trade name was *Dyna* – was marketed from 1942 as a meat substitute. It was made from brewer's yeast and vegetable fat. With the end of war rationing in the 1950s, pork liver was added and it became 'Le Parfait'.

Current packaging is decorated with the Matterhorn and the Swiss cross.

Rivella

- In 1951, the Swiss entrepreneur Robert Barth founded the company *Rivella* to commercialise a whey-based drink, using a recipe devised by a biologist from the canton of Zug.

  In 1957, the product was introduced to the Netherlands, the only other country where it is well-known.

- The main ingredient of Rivella is whey and the marketing for the product focuses on health and sport, as well as on Switzerland, well known for its milk production.

The origin of the name 'Rivella' is the Italian word for 'revelation' ('rive-lazione'). 'Ricola' is the acronym of 'Richterich & Co. Laufen', which was the original name of the manufacturer. The name 'Ovomal-tine' references some of the ingredients of the product (eggs and malt). The name 'Cenovis' derives from an amalgam of the Latin words 'cenare' ('to eat') and 'vis' ('strength').

Ricola

The recipe for Ricola was developed in Laufen (canton of Basel-Land-schaft – Basel 'Country') in 1940. Today it is exported to some 50 countries and is marketed with strong reference to its Swiss origins. Humorous advertising spots under the slogan 'Who invented it?' ('*Wer hat's erfunden?*' in German) feature Mexicans, Chinese, or even Eskimos claiming that Ricola is theirs, and then being reminded by a Swiss arriving on the scene of the real origin of the product.

In the US ads for Ricola, alphorns, the Matterhorn and yodelling are featured; in France other Swiss stereotypes are used, like cleanliness or slowness.

→ **Chocolate** (poster, 1960s)

At the end of the 19th and in the first half of the 20th century, colonial references, sometimes overtly racist, were widely used by chocolate manufacturers in many countries. Since the Swiss speciality was milk chocolate, local producers placed more emphasis on alpine themes. This advertisement for the Maestrani brand from St. Gallen is an exception.

↓ **Chocolate** (contemporary metal plaque)

This reproduction of an advertisement that probably dates to the early 20th century is viewed today as a decorative item. The original image uses a mountain theme and all that is associated with it (cow, shepherd, chalet and pasture) in order to sell the chocolate. Swiss products gradually moved the aesthetic approach in this direction, and it has now replaced the earlier colonial imagery.

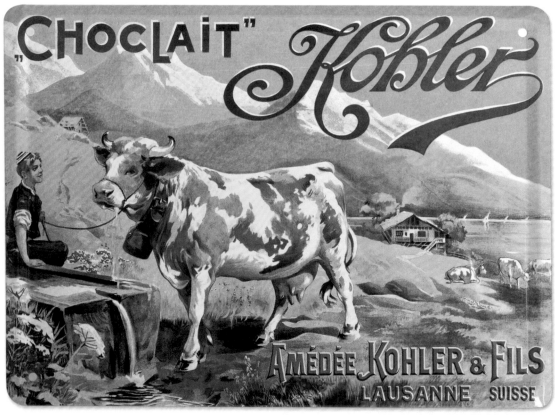

← **Cheese** (photograph, 1993)

The Swiss skier, Urs Lehmann (here with a team-mate) wins the downhill race at the world championships in Morioka, Japan, on 5 February 1993, wearing the famous ski-suit sponsored by the Swiss Cheese Union.

↑ **Cheese** (postage stamp, 2000)   ↑↗ **The Swiss Army knife** (postage stamps, 2006)

Stamps are among the most collected items in the world. Moreover, their official status gives a special aura to the subjects depicted on them, as a kind of consecration. Fondue and the Swiss Army knife (in its non-military and first military versions) are here considered as national icons.

→ **The Swiss Army knife** (cartoon, 2009)

In this cartoon linking the Swiss Army knife with the vote banning the construction of minarets in Switzerland, Michel Kichka, an Israeli cartoonist, provides one of many examples of the association between the Swiss Army knife and its country of origin.

Buildings and events

A CHALET
↓

AN IMITATION CHALET
(BUNKER)
↓

National fairs

These events, six of which have been organised since 1883, offered – according to the spirit of each period – an idealised image of Switzerland.

The painting *Panorama of the Swiss Alps,* one of the main attractions of the Geneva National Fair, was 17 metres high and 114 metres long. Its owner had already exhibited it in Vincennes (1892), Chicago (1893) and Antwerp (1894). After Geneva it continued on to the World Fair in Paris in 1900 and to Dublin in 1903, where it was destroyed by heavy storm.

Six editions

- So far six national fairs have been organised in Switzerland: Zurich, 1883; Geneva, 1896; Bern, 1914; Zurich again, 1939 (the so-called *Landi*); Lausanne, 1964 (*Expo64*) and in the 'Three Lakes' region (Neuchatel, Bienne and Morat), 2002 (*Expo.02*).

- The original reason for mounting national fairs was an economic one, as they provided an opportunity for Swiss companies to **showcase** their activities at national and even international level. However, it quickly became obvious that they also played a powerful role in the realm of symbols and national identity.

The national fairs were very popular. In 1883, 1.7 million tickets were sold; in 1896, 2.3 million; in 1914, 3.2 million; in 1939, 10.5 million; in 1964, 11.7 million; and in 2002, 10.3 million.

The Doerfli

- The main attraction of the 1896 Geneva national fair was the **Swiss village**. A replica of an alpine village was built, complete with streets, shops and houses, sometimes using 'recycled' mountain chalets.

An artificial mountain was set up next to the village. In its hollow centre the vast Panorama of the Swiss Alps was exhibited.

- In 1900, the *Doerfli* (as it was known to Swiss German-speakers) represented Switzerland at the Paris World Fair, where it caused a sensation and, until 1939, would be considered an essential component of such events.

None of the Doerfli reproduced a real Swiss village. Rather, they brought together various elements of Swiss architecture, with particular reference to the rural habitat.

- The *Doerfli* was inhabited by actors in traditional costume (p.104) and projected an image of an alpine Switzerland. It was an **allegory of the country**: a little island where ancestral customs were protected. This vision of things was at one with the basic purpose of the national fairs: it was clear that it did not match any specific economic or social reality in a country that was becoming increasingly industrialised and urban, but it provided the population with a unifying sense of identity through a perception of themselves based in fantasy and myth.

An archive of images

- With the exception of the first in 1883, which preceded the first motion pictures in the 1890s, national fairs have always maintained close links with **film-making**. The 1896 (and 1900) Swiss Village was filmed by the Lumière Brothers and their competitors. In 1896, at the Geneva fair, the very first Swiss film productions were shown.

  In Zurich in 1939, there were some thirty displays showing films. In Lausanne in 1964, there were several advanced cinema installations, including the nine circular screens of the 'Circarama'. Expo.02 commissioned a large number of films, notably from art and cinema schools.

- In a more general sense, the national fairs always invested major resources in the presentation of a **wide variety of images**, using the technology of the time – prints, photography, film, video, etc. All these apparently unrelated images, whether artistic, for entertainment or for technical demonstration purposes, actually form a single 'image': each time they reflected an **idealised view** of Switzerland.

Like the 1896 fair, *Expo.02* also exhibited a panorama, this time of the battle of Morat. Designed by the architect Jean Nouvel it was housed in a floating structure ('Le Monolithe') on the Morat lake. It had been painted at the same period as the *Panorama of the Swiss Alps,* exhibited a century earlier, but had been rolled-up and not been publicly viewed for many years. Major restoration work was required for its display in 2002.

Posters

- The posters of the national fairs were their **visiting cards**. In view of the importance of these events in terms of national identity, they are also visiting cards for Switzerland at any given moment.

- The posters for the first two national fairs are a faithful reflection of the national iconography of the late 19th century: they depict allegorical figures, overburdened with symbols, like the shepherd playing the alphorn (1883) and Helvetia (1896).

- From 1964, the posters depict more nuanced symbols of identity and some even do without them. The exaggerated chauvinism of the 1920s and 1930s in some countries led to a more reserved approach to such heavily loaded imagery, even in relation to Switzerland. Artistic creations and other means were used to promote the homeland.

The Swiss chalet

The chalet is considered to be the quintessential Swiss residence. However, very few Swiss actually live in chalets and the best known of them often belong to rich foreigners.

Originally simple rural buildings, chalets have sometimes become luxury residences. In Gstaad, Ernesto Bertarelli's chalet cost 30 million Francs; it held the world record for chalet prices until it was surpassed by the one purchased for 100 million Francs by the Greek shipowner Peter Livanos, also in Gstaad.

Part of the scenery

- Originally, a chalet was an **isolated rural building**, normally at medium or high altitudes. The chalet got its name several centuries ago in the French-speaking part of Switzerland ('chalet' is a corrupted version of the pre-Roman word *cala*, meaning 'a shelter'). It was only in the 19th century that the word spread to the whole of Switzerland.

Today, the word chalet exists in most European languages: das Chalet, the chalet, el chalet, il chalet, etc.

- The **aesthetic mutation** of chalets was linked to romantic ideas about mountains and alpine scenery, beginning in the 17th, but most marked in the 19th century. At that time, the development of tourism, alpine exploration and mountain-climbing – together with the search for common values of identity – raised the level of interest in mountains and their inhabitants, and thus the buildings in which they lived.

- **Authors** of the 'Age of Enlightenment', like Jean-Jacques Rousseau (1772–1778), idealised the chalet, which was seen as a simple rustic home close to nature.

Chalets are also mentioned by Swiss authors, such as Jeremias Gotthelf (1797–1854) and Gottfried Keller (1819–1890).

- **Landscape artists** adopted the chalet as a theme, just as they did for thatched cottages, windmills, ruins and bridges. The little wooden house became almost obligatory for representations of alpine scenery.

There are many chalets in the work of the French painter Louis Etienne Watelet (1780–1866) and the Swiss painters Alexandre Calame (1810–1864) and Auguste Baud-Bovy (1848–1899).

Something for tourists

• At the end of the 19th century, the sending of **postcards** became more widespread in Switzerland; in 1871, the postal services began delivery of postcards. This means of communication rapidly became very popular in Switzerland, already a popular tourist destination. The chalet, as a typical component of the Swiss landscape, was one of the favourite images depicted on postcards.

In 1900, more than 50 million postcards were handled by the Swiss postal service.

• In view of the success of postcards, the tourist business expanded its activities to allow visitors various opportunities to take home 'a little piece of Switzerland' in the form of **miniature reproductions** of all kinds. From the end of the 19th century, many **souvenir** shops in Switzerland sold miniature chalets in porcelain and wood in addition to musical boxes and snow globes. The chalet, no longer much resembling a traditional home, is one of the first images that comes to mind when foreigners talk about Switzerland.

Use and abuse

• The notion of 'the Swiss chalet', as a **symbol of an enhanced natural landscape**, was already widespread outside Switzerland at the end of the 19th century. Many builders, in Switzerland and abroad, advertised pre-fabricated chalets. They were not specifically designed for the mountains and often ended up in the residential suburbs of large cities.

This trend did not please everyone and became part of what was considered 'bad taste' or 'kitsch' in relation to the design of chalets, especially when they were not built in the mountains or were in an urban setting. In his Voyage en Espagne (1843), Théophile Gautier noted with horror that in the Retiro Park in Madrid 'there is above all else a chalet that is one of the most ridiculous and comic things imaginable.'

• The **English,** who comprised the majority of tourists in Switzerland in the 19th century, were especially fond of the Swiss landscape and its chalets. Queen Victoria had one built in the park of Osborne House on the Isle of Wight, and filled it with Swiss furniture and decorations. Built in 1850, it is still in perfect condition.

The English novelist, Charles Dickens, also ordered a chalet (from a Parisian company). He had it built in 1865 in Gad's Hill Park, Kent, as a place for him to write.

In 1910–1911, near the entrance to Glacier National Park in Montana, the *Belton Chalets* were built on the Swiss model as accommodation for tourists visiting the reserve. By the mid-20th century they were no longer in use, but were restored in 1997 and subsequently converted into a hotel and restaurant. In 2000, they were registered as a *National Historic Landmark*, a designation that is given to sites in the USA that are considered to be of national historic interest.

Bunkers and bomb shelters

Bunkers and bomb shelters have been linked to the image of Switzerland since the 1940s. Their rapid spread has made them into a symbol of the defensive neutrality of the country.

From ramparts to reinforced concrete

- In the Middle Ages, Switzerland – like most European countries – had a multitude of castles, among which some, such as Chillon (····} p. 83) would become famous.

- More modern fortifications, built to resist cannon shot and designed by specialist engineers, appeared at the time of the Thirty Years War (1618–1648).

- During the first World War, the army constructed several fortifications in Switzerland and – from 1934 (influenced by the Maginot line) – put up a series of defensive posts along the frontiers.

  Prior to the 1939 mobilisation, many national fortifications did not yet have the symbolic significance they would subsequently acquire.

A BOMB SHELTER CAN BE USEFUL FOR AN INVASION ...

... OF REFUGEES!

The national redoubt

- From the summer of 1940, the 'national redoubt' was at the heart of General Guisan's defence policy (····} p. 40). The mountainous regions were to be fortified – the frontiers and the lower regions would not be secured.

- The aim was to deter potential invaders. Once these regions had been fortified, they would be able to resist longer and would increase the enemy's losses.

  There was much criticism of the plan because the enemy would nevertheless have been able to occupy the cities and industrial sites.

- The national redoubt consisted of a series of underground fortifications, enhancing Switzerland's reputation as a fortress. In addition to the works that were visible, such as anti-tank obstacles (sometimes called 'Toblerones'), some of the constructions were ingeniously hidden in the mountainous heart of the country, an area already steeped in symbolism. Subject to secrecy regulations, they have been a source of fascination – and sometimes false ideas – for several generations.

  This fortification policy was abandoned at the end of the Cold War.

The 'Swiss square' was a typical infantry combat formation in the Middle Ages. It looked like a **human box**, with protruding spears and halberds.

- The national redoubt symbolised a sovereign and independent Switzerland, determined to resist and defend itself; it became an essential part of national identity.

Fallout shelters

- From 1963, when the fixation on atomic war was at its most intense, the Swiss government required the cellars of all newly built houses to be equipped with a shelter against atomic attack.

- The spread of these private shelters, nothing special for the Swiss, was noted with interest by foreigners. It became part of the image of Switzerland abroad.

By 2006, 300,000 shelters had been built in the cellars of private houses, together with 5100 community shelters. These provided room for 8.6 million people, more than the total population of Switzerland.

- Norway had a shelter construction programme similar to Switzerland's, but cancelled it in 1998. It may reasonably be asked whether the Swiss shelters were genuinely useful.

In 2005, Pierre Kohler, a Member of Parliament from the Jura, put forward a bill that would have abolished the requirement for a fallout shelter in private homes. However, the Federal Council maintained that they served a useful purpose. Since 2011, new home owners have the alternative of paying a fixed financial contribution (based on the size of the household) to the theoretical cost of places in a community shelter.

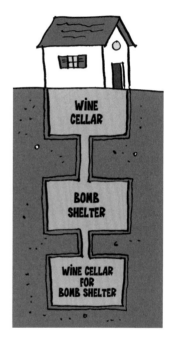

Conversion to other uses

Many bunkers and several fallout shelters are no longer used for their original purpose. Some of these, with particular architectural features, can be put to different uses:

- use as a museum is the most obvious (e.g. the fortress of Pré-Giroud, near Vallorbe in the canton of Vaud and the bunker in the town of Gland on the 'Toblerone path');
- two bunkers in the Bernese Oberland – re-christened *Swiss Fort Knox* – are being used by a private company as highly secured data centres;
- a bunker in the St. Gotthard mountain has become an enormous secured warehouse;
- a fallout shelter in Teufen (canton of Aargau) was converted into a 'no-star' hotel (its name is, indeed, *Null Stern Hotel*): it has only communal bathrooms and there are no windows or heating.
- it is planned to convert the military fortress of Chillon, close to the famous castle and the vineyards of Lavaux, into a prestigious wine-cellar for visits and tastings.

Since the end of the Cold War, nearly 7000 military fortifications have been privatised or sold to communities (as in the case of Gland).

With a capacity of up to 20,000, the Sonnenberg tunnel (in the canton of Lucerne) was home to the largest fallout shelter in the world. Its one and a half metre thick doors weighed 350 metric tons. It was demolished in 2006.

Transport

Means of transport in Switzerland are linked to other components of Swiss identity, such as punctuality and the landscape; by bringing the different parts of the territory together and facilitating the development of the national economy, they contributed to the modernisation of Switzerland.

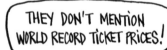

THEY DON'T MENTION WORLD RECORD TICKET PRICES!

SBB

In 1850, a journey between Milan and Basel took about 50 hours. Most of the route could be covered by stage-coach, but travellers had to take a train between Milan and Camerlata and then a boat between Flüelen and Lucerne. Today it is a four-hour train journey.

Postal buses

- The story of the postal buses begins with the setting up of a network of stagecoaches in **1849**.

  The Gotthard mail coach is the most famous. The opening of the railway tunnel in 1882 led to its withdrawal and a song was composed in its honour: Der letzte Postillon vom Gotthard ('The last Gotthard mail coach'). Today, the stagecoach service is back as a tourist attraction.

- In 1906, a postal vehicle ran between Bern and Detligen (canton of Bern). Other itineraries were added – especially after the first World War – to reach parts of the country not accessible by rail. Since then, these yellow buses have become part of Swiss mountain imagery.

  Since 1923, the mountain postal buses have a horn with a three-note combination, C#, E and A, that feature in Rossini's overture to his opera William Tell.

- Today, there are some 2200 postal buses, servicing a 11,000 kilometre network and carrying some **139 million passengers** a year.

The Federal Railways

- Railway construction started late in Switzerland. The first connection, between Zurich and Baden (canton of Aargau), was opened in 1847.

  In England, the first line was opened to the public in 1825.

- At first, the network was owned by a few private companies; their finances were not sound and they were unable to provide a service that met the needs of a rapidly industrialising nation. After lengthy political debates, these companies were nationalised in **1902** to form the Swiss Federal Railways (CFF in French, SBB in German and FFS in Italian).

- Since then, trains have become a standard form of transport for the Swiss. According to figures published by the International Union of Railways in 2008, an inhabitant of Switzerland takes the train on average 50 times a year, a European record. Switzerland leads the world in the per capita total of kilometres travelled by rail.

Swissair

- The airline company that represented Switzerland until 2002 was founded in **1931**. It grew in size after the second World War, extending its network and increasing its fleet. It was a source of national pride.

Swissair hostesses were frequently featured in Swiss magazines.

In 1934, Nelly Diener joined the staff of Swissair and became the first air hostess in Europe. Her career was short, as she died on 28 February 1936 in the crash of a Douglas DC-2 at Düben-dorf, Swissair's first accident.

- In 2001 the company went through a serious crisis that led to its bankruptcy. The fuel companies halted supplies and its planes were grounded. This **grounding** was experienced as a national humiliation.

On 2 October 2001, the anchor of the Swiss German TV News announced in funereal tones: 'Swissair is grounded and will remain there.'

- Despite its status as a private company, the federal Council decided to provide 2 billion Francs of public funds to save Swissair. This controversial decision shows the symbolic importance of the company for the country. Even after these measures, Swissair's bankruptcy was declared on 31 March 2002. A new company – **Swiss** – was created from Swissair's ashes, but does not have the prestige of its predecessor, in particular because it was subsequently taken over by the German *Lufthansa*.

These events were covered in a 2006 Swiss film directed by Michael Steiner: 'Grounding – the last days of Swissair'.

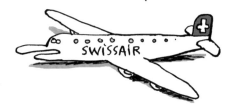

'Belle Epoque' steamers

- Steam navigation on Swiss lakes began on the Lac Léman in **1823** with the commissioning of the *William Tell*. Despite this patriotic name, an American was behind the project. Soon afterwards, other steamers were launched on the Neuchatel and Zurich lakes. In 1905, nearly 250 **paddle** and propeller steamers operated on Swiss lakes, of which 60 were exclusively for cargo.

- Although no longer technologically in tune with the times, several paddle-steamers have been preserved alongside more modern vessels; they have style and are a tourist attraction. In 2011, the Belle Epoque steamers of the Lac Léman were designated as **historical monuments**.

In terms of passenger capacity, the Swiss fleet of Belle Epoque steamers leads the world.

↑↗ National Fairs (posters, 1914)

These two posters were created for the 1914 National Fair in Bern. The first, initially chosen as the official poster, was the work of the painter Emil Cardinaux, who was inspired by Ferdinand Hodler. When published, it was widely criticised: the newspaper *La Patrie Suisse* used the words 'flashy impudence' and 'overweight draft-horse' – and another design was commissioned from Plinio Colombi, who decided to show the Jungfrau peak, a more federating symbol.

↓↘ The Swiss chalet (posters, 1940s)

Rather than showing the scenery or the various sporting activities available (skiing, skating, mountain-climbing), the resort of Davos, in Graubünden, chose the chalet for its tourism promotion: it embodies, on its own, in summer as in winter, the 'mountain spirit'.

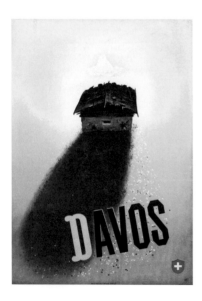 

↑ **The Swiss chalet** (poster, 1930)

This advertisement was made to promote the sale of prefabricated chalets, which was already flourishing by the mid-19th century, and places the chalet – logically – in alpine scenery. Many of these chalets were actually put up in city residential suburbs.

IRGENDWO IN DER SCHWEIZ + QUELQUE PART EN SUISSE
Beton-Bunker Im Felsen. + Fortin en béton coulé dans le rocher.

← **Bunkers and bomb shelters** (postcard, 1940s)

This propaganda illustration from the period of the general mobilisation shows the construction of a bunker 'somewhere in Switzerland'. This description reflects the secrecy in which the actual construction of the 'national redoubt' was shrouded: it was promoted, but without giving away any details.

→ **Bunkers and bomb shelters**
(modern photograph)

The entrance to the Pré-Giroud fortress, built near Vallorbe between 1937 and 1939, was camouflaged behind what appears to be a chalet. This building, typical for Swiss meadows, was supposed to blend the fortress into the scenery.

↑ Means of transport (poster, 1890)

This advertisement for the Jura-Simplon railway pre-dates the creation of the Federal Railways in 1902. Clearly intended for foreign visitors, it places the train in the middle of a reconstituted landscape, comprising an impressive collection of Swiss symbols.

Places

The Matterhorn

A rocky pyramid with an easily identifiable shape, the Matterhorn is located between Switzerland and Italy. At 4478 metres, it is the twelfth highest peak in the Alps, but by far the best known.

The logo of Paramount Pictures Corporation shows a mountain peak, surrounded by stars, that is sometimes taken to be the Matterhorn, because the resemblance is close. In fact, the shape is much closer to that of Artesonraju, in the Peruvian Andes. Moreover, the shape on the logo has been altered over time.

A mountain-climbing myth

- The lively history of the conquest of the Matterhorn in the 19th century partly explains its reputation. In **1865**, after several unsuccessful attempts, two expeditions set off for the summit at almost exactly the same moment; **Whymper**, an Englishman, from the Swiss side; and **Carrel**, an Italian, from the other. The challenge was not only symbolic in relation to the mountain but involved national identity, as this was the period of Italian unification and Carrel had set himself the objective of conquering it for the new Italy.

- In the end, it was Whymper who won, but his victory was marked by tragedy: during the descent, one of the team slipped and dragged three others to their deaths in the fall.
This accident was widely reported abroad and inspired several films.

- Today, the ascent of the Matterhorn is commonplace, and some 1000 to 1500 climbers reach the summit every year.
On some days, there can be up to a hundred climbers near the summit.

The unconquerable

- In **1906**, two engineers submitted to the Federal Ministry of Posts and Railways a plan for a railway line ending only 20 metres from the summit.

- Their daring plan proposed two tracks: an **electric cog-railway** from the bottom to a hut at 3052 metres; and then an underground funicular (almost a lift) bringing passengers to the top.

- The plan was violently opposed and never saw the light of day. The mountain was already part of national mythology and the proposal was seen as a violation of its status. A joint petition by the Swiss Alpine Club and the *Schweizer Heimatschutz* (an association set up to protect the natural and built 'heritage' of Switzerland) collected 70,000 signatures.
Intellectuals and journalists contributed to the dispute (translations):
– 'Who will we find in this alpine bar? That vulgar band of pretentious and impatient tourists, with no culture, no respect and no education, unable to appreciate simple things, noisy people who understand only cut-price luxury.' (Ernest Bovet)
– 'The Matterhorn belongs to the Swiss people. We cannot tolerate that this beautiful common heritage be handed over to a few, purely for the sake of profit.' (Marius Gos)
– 'Even if they are invisible, the lift and the constructions at the summit will be for the Matterhorn like a blemish on a beautiful body.' (Raymond de Girard)

A tourist icon

- The Matterhorn is inextricably linked to the image of **Zermatt**. It was the fame of the Matterhorn that made Zermatt one of the main tourist sites in Switzerland.

- In the mid-19th century, shortly before the conquest of the Matterhorn, Zermatt opened to hotels and tourism, but only during the summer. The small, impoverished village, comprising only 369 inhabitants in 1850, has now grown into a tourist resort of renown, with a local population of 6000 and a tourist capacity of 17,000.

  There is a museum in Zermatt devoted solely to the Matterhorn. Among the exhibits is the equipment used for the first ascent in 1865.

- The view of the Matterhorn from Zermatt is familiar to the whole world. From the Italian resort of Cervinia on the other side, however, the mountain is hardly recognisable, and it is the former that has become a **symbol of Switzerland**.

  The silhouette of the mountain and signs with the names 'Matterhorn' and 'Cervin' are omnipresent in Zermatt. The Matterhorn is available in all shapes and sizes in souvenir shops throughout Switzerland.

- There is a 'second' Matterhorn in **Disneyland** in California (the oldest theme park in the world, opened in 1955). It is 400 times smaller than the real thing but is still impressive and carries the fame of the mountain to the cradle of the film industry.

An advertising icon

- In 1990, Yvan Hostettler authored a book entitled *Cervin, montagne de pub* ('The Matterhorn, a mountain of publicity'), in which he listed some of the publicity campaigns that have used the mountain. He mentions that the Matterhorn is used not only to evoke Switzerland (it appears, for example, in advertisements for a Portuguese chocolate named Suidzo), but also for its association with fresh air (mentholated sweets and air-conditioning units) and purity (publicity for mineral water).

- Marketing often requires images that rapidly create targeted associations in the minds of consumers. The recurring use of the Matterhorn confirms its privileged position in the public's imagination, and not only in Switzerland.

In 1988, a commercial venture was put forward to illuminate the Matterhorn as if it was a historic building. Like the 1906 railway proposal, this idea – which hardly made sense in terms of energy consumption – was abandoned.

AND I THOUGHT THE DISNEYLAND MATTERHORN WAS DIFFICULT!

The Rütli

The Rütli meadows over-looking Lake Lucerne are the most important patriotic site in Switzerland.

When the Swiss Guards at the Vatican swear the oath of allegiance, they raise their right hand with three fingers extended. These symbolise the Holy Trinity and are not related to the Rütli oath. However, the three Swiss would certainly have sworn their oath in the same way.

After their election, the members of the Swiss Federal Council – unless they choose a non-religious form of oath-taking – swear an oath in the same fashion.

The three Swiss

- The *Rütli* (*Grütli* in French and Italian) is the place where, according to myth, Walter Fürst of Uri, Werner Stauffacher of Schwyz and Arnold von Melchtal of Unterwald swore an oath of mutual assistance against the Habsburgs. This **legendary oath** is viewed as one of the defining moments in the creation of Switzerland.

- Since the late Middle Ages, the Rütli oath has been a source of inspiration for artists. In the 19th century, painters and sculptors, in search of symbols of identity, adopted the theme and gave form to the representation of three men linking their left hands and raising their right with **three fingers extended**. This image became popularised and was used on a wide variety of objects, from pewter plates to postcards.

'The Three Swiss' is a common name for local pubs in Switzerland.

The Swiss national day

- According to the 16th century historian Aegidius Tschudi, the Rütli oath was sworn on 8 November 1307 and, until the 19th century, this date was celebrated as the founding date of the Confederation. In the early 19th century, an older pact was discovered, signed at the beginning of August **1291**, and this became the new date.

- The Swiss national day has only been celebrated since 1891, the 600th anniversary of the Confederation. It was then that the precise date of **1 August** was fixed.

This arbitrary choice may have been made to compete with the first of May, which trade unions and parties of the left began to celebrate at this time.

- Some journalists disagreed with this official decision, maintaining that 8 November should have been chosen because it was already well established in people's minds.

- The annual celebration of the first of August began in 1899 at the request of the Swiss community abroad which – in contrast to their host countries – had no national day.

On the 700th anniversary in 1991, a referendum was initiated by the Schweizer Demokraten, a right-wing party, to have the first of August declared as a public holiday. It was accepted by an 83.8% majority.

The 'cradle of the nation'

- The Rütli has been the scene of many **patriotic, political and symbolic events**, each hoping to benefit from its aura.

- In 1780, Guillaume Raynal, the French philosopher, suggested that a monument to freedom should be built there, a proposal that did not encounter much enthusiasm on the part of the authorities of Uri. In 1789, the latter adopted a plan for a memorial but later abandoned the project.

- In 1859, a private company drew up a plan for a hotel on the site. To prevent this 'profanation', the *Société Suisse d'utilité publique*, an association set up to promote issues of public interest, purchased the meadow for 55,000 Francs, to be raised by public subscription (which actually brought in 95,000 Francs) and donated it to the Confederation the following year.

- Since 1860, an annual marksmanship competition has been organised at the Rütli on the Wednesday before St. Martin's day in November.

- In 1884, to cope with the growth in the number of visitors to the site, a regular steamer service was inaugurated.

- In 1940, General Guisan (····⫸ p. 40) held a meeting with some 400 senior army officers on the site and made an appeal for unconditional resistance against an invader.

- Since 2006, security at the Rütli site on the first of August is reinforced to prevent disturbances by extreme right-wing groups meeting there on the Swiss national day.

- Every year some 100,000 people visit the Rütli.

In 2007, Ueli Maurer, the Chairman of the SVP/UDC party, described the Rütli as 'a simple meadow with a few cowpats here and there'. In 2011, senior members of his party gathered there for a 'Rütli report' that declared that 'the European Union is the opposite of the guiding principle of the Rütli.'

Tourist attractions

Swiss scenery could be considered a tourist attraction in itself; indeed, its very variety makes it impossible to narrow it down to a single image. However, in addition to the Matterhorn, there are a few other places that are also very much in evidence on postcards and in tourist guides.

The stories of five people who fell into the bear pit in Bern found their way into the 'Miscellaneous News' in the press. Of these, only one survived: a doctor from the Italian part of Switzerland – he was drunk and fell in while throwing snowballs at the bears and was saved by the bear-keeper.

The giant fountain in Geneva

• Originally, the Geneva fountain was not designed as a tourist attraction: a hydraulic factory was built in **1886** on the river Rhône to provide electricity to the city's manufacturing units and released excess water pressure at night when the workshops were closed. Nevertheless, its height of some 30 metres was noticed by tourists.

• In 1891, the 600th anniversary of the Confederation, a more impressive replica, actually designed as a tourist attraction, was built on the lake shore where it still stands. This fountain reached a height of 90 metres, increased to **140 metres** in 1951.

The Geneva fountain is not the highest in the world: this is located in Jeddah in Saudi Arabia and is 312 metres high. The fountain in Seoul, built for the 2002 FIFA World Cup, reaches 202 metres.

The Bern bear pit

• A bear is the symbol of the city of Bern and appears on the **crest and coat of arms** of the canton. According to legend, Duke Berthold V of Zähringen founded the city in 1191 after killing a bear (*Bär* in German). This episode inspired the name of the future federal capital city.

• The first record of bears in captivity in Bern dates to 1441. Several pits have been built since. The last, completed in 1857, is empty today: in 2009, the city of Bern decided that it was not an appropriate habitat for the animals and moved them to a more comfortable space, the famous ***Bärenpark***, situated next to the disused pit on the banks of the Aar.

The Castle of Chillon

- This "mass of towers on a mass of rocks," as Victor Hugo described it, is a favourite of writers, poets and painters in search of romantic and picturesque locations.

The castle features in Lord Byron's poem The Prisoner of Chillon, *which describes the fate of François Bonivard, held captive there in the 16th century.*

- Appearing on a multiplicity of products, the castle soon became a major tourist attraction; its popularity was helped by the proximity of the town of Montreux which was already a tourist destination in the 19th century (between 1850 and 1900, the number of hotels there increased from 8 to 70).

300,000 tourists visit the castle each year.

The Aletsch Glacier

- Covering some 120 km², the Aletsch is the **largest glacier in the Alps**. Its fame was due to the development of mountain-climbing, and subsequently to alpine tourism. The Swiss Alpine Club created an access path in the 19th century and several mountain huts were set up to provide accommodation for hikers and mountaineers, including the famous Concordia hut, built in 1870.

- In 1912, the construction of the Jungfrau railway made the Glacier more accessible.

In 2001, UNESCO recognised Eiger, Mönch, Jungfrau and the Aletsch glacier as a World Heritage site.

The Lucerne bridge

- Built in 1333, the ***Kapellbrücke*** (Chapel Bridge) is the oldest covered wooden bridge in Europe. Its picturesque design, with angles and turrets, is easily recognisable.

- With its hundred or so 17th century triangular paintings, showing the history of Switzerland in general and Lucerne in particular, the bridge is also a picture gallery.

- Several fires over time resulted in the partial destruction of the bridge. On the last occasion, in 1993, several paintings were lost and have been replaced by copies.

Lucerne, deprived of its symbol, managed to replace the bridge in only eight months.

The nine hundred UNESCO World Heritage sites are usually attractive for tourists. Switzerland has ten of them. In addition to the Jungfrau area, there is also Monte San Giorgio in Ticino, the Piz Sardona (situated between Graubünden, Glaris and St. Gallen), the old town of Bern, the Müstair convent in Graubünden, the convent in St. Gallen, the castles in Bellinzona, the wine-growing region of Lavaux above the Lac Léman in the canton of Vaud, the Rhaetian railway between the Albula and Bernina passes in Graubünden, and the watchmaking towns of La-Chaux-de-Fonds and Le Locle.

↑ The Matterhorn (poster, 1904)

This advertisement for Zermatt makes full use of the Matterhorn, as does most of the other promotional material for the resort. Zermatt's success is very closely related to the presence of the Matterhorn in the surrounding landscape.

↗ The Matterhorn (various items, 1990–2011)

The Matterhorn, as a national emblem, tourist symbol or advertising icon, is used on a wide variety of items, both official and unofficial. In the 1990s, even Coca-Cola temporarily abandoned its American identity to use the Matterhorn on a lapel pin.

→ The Matterhorn (postcard, 1950s)

This postcard was printed to promote a Swiss restaurant in Chicago. Several national symbols are at work here, including – of course – the Matterhorn, which was painted on a wall inside.

↑ The Rütli (postcard, 1914)

The Rütli oath features in the play *Tell*, first performed at the Théâtre du Jorat in Mézières (canton of Vaud) in 1914. The scenery – inspired by the work of Ferdinand Hodler – shows the Rütli meadows. Just as in the 19th century, the 'three Swiss' swear the oath clasping each other's left hand with three right-hand fingers extended.

→→ The Rütli (postcards, approx. 1910 and 1932)

The first postcard shows one of the companions of the 'three Swiss'. Their oath is illustrated in the background in its classic form. On the other hand, the second postcard shows an oath more in tune with the period of its publication; the three fingers are abandoned in favour of a fascist-like salute.

→ Tourist attractions (photo, 2010)

On the occasion of the Swiss national day in 2010, the Chillon castle was decorated with a light-show of Swiss crosses. The castle, a symbol of tourism in French-speaking Switzerland, was thus joined with national symbolism – despite the fact that the original castle was actually built by the House of Savoy.

Know-how

Watchmaking

Watchmaking may not be the most important industrial activity in Switzerland, but it is certainly the most typical and an essential component of the country's reputation abroad.

Most people would say that watchmaking holds pride of place in Swiss industrial activity. However, the export figures of the mechanical engineering and chemical industries are higher.

Origins of the tradition

- The know-how for watchmaking came to Geneva as of 1550 with the **Huguenots**, Protestant refugees fleeing persecution in France. In the **17th century**, watchmaking spread to the Jura mountains and, in the 19th, to Bern and Solothurn.

- Swiss watches are essentially **export** products and rapidly acquired an international reputation; in the 18th century they were already prized in Asia and America.

In 1870, three out of four watches produced in the world were Swiss.

- At the end of the 20th century, Switzerland was still the leading manufacturer of watches in terms of value (50%), but Asian producers had become the undisputed leaders in terms of quantity; today, 80% of watches are made in China.

The Cuckoo clock

- The cuckoo clock is seen as one of the most typical Swiss products.

In the film The Third Man *(produced by Carol Reed in 1949), Harry Lime, played by Orson Welles, says famously: 'You know what the fellow said – in Italy, for thirty years under the Borgias, they had warfare, terror, murder and bloodshed, but they produced Michelangelo, Leonardo da Vinci and the Renaissance. In Switzerland, they had brotherly love, they had five hundred years of democracy and peace – and what did that produce? The cuckoo clock.'*

SWISS GERMAN CUCKOO
↓

GRÜEZI!

- Originally, however, the cuckoo clock was **not a Swiss invention**: its production began in the Black Forest area of Germany in the 18th century. It was its shape as a chalet that led foreigners to conclude that this wall clock was a typically Swiss product. It is omnipresent in souvenir shops in various designs decorated with the Swiss cross, Edelweiss and figures wearing traditional costume.

Some cuckoo clocks are made in Switzerland, but most of the low-price models are Asian imports.

The label 'Swiss Made'

- The label 'Swiss Made' may only be used on watches if at least **50% of the value** is manufactured in Switzerland. The determining factor is thus value and not the amount of labour required for manufacture.

Some 'Swiss Made' watches may have spent more time in the hands of workers abroad (where labour costs are lower) than in Switzerland.

International marketing

- Swiss watches are essentially produced for export and major marketing initiatives have been undertaken to promote sales abroad. The industry has been present at all the World Fairs, beginning in 1851 in London.

- These international campaigns were intensified after the second World War. Advertisements for Swiss watches were placed in US magazines. At that time, the emphasis was often on relatively cheap watches, the origin of which was more important than the brand name.

The Swiss watchmaking industry also places advertisements in the collective name of 'The Watchmakers of Switzerland'.

- Sponsorship of well-publicised events is an integral part of the promotion of Swiss watches.

For example: major sporting events at which the time-keeping is done by a Swiss manufacturer; the first solo transatlantic flight by Charles Lindbergh in 1927; and the first lunar landing mission of the Apollo 11 spacecraft in 1969.

MR. WANG, I'M STILL WAITING FOR YOUR DELIVERY OF WATCHES 'MADE IN SWITZERLAND'.

SWISS WATCHES

During the Apollo 11 space mission, Buzz Aldrin, the second man to walk on the moon, was wearing a Swiss watch: an Omega Speedmaster chronograph. The first man on the moon, Neil Armstrong, left his watch on board as a back-up in case the spacecraft's clock failed.

The plastic phenomenon

- The 1975 **economic crisis**, combined with the arrival of Asian quartz watches, almost killed off the Swiss watchmaking industry. It looked as if only a few prestigious brand names could survive.

- The solution did not, however, come from the high-end market. Designed in 1980 and brought to market in 1983, the **Swatch** (shortened form of *Swiss Watch*) was 'trendy', cheap and Swiss Made.

The first model, the GB 101, was entirely black, but Swatch rapidly began offering a wide range of colours and designs, always emphasising the Swiss origin of the watch.

Banking

Financial activity is a major contributor to Swiss economic prosperity; however, it does not always help Switzerland's image abroad.

In Nazi Germany, maintaining an illegal bank account in Switzerland was a capital crime: for example, the Nazi regime sent agents to Zurich to collect information that led to the execution in 1934 of three citizens of the Reich.

A little history

- In the 16th century, while most European States were heavily in debt, Swiss cities had generally sound finances. Trade was flourishing and capital was accumulating. It was at this time that some merchants began to specialise in lending and set up networks abroad.

  In 1789, some forty Swiss bankers were active in France.

- In the 19th century, **cantonal banks** and some large **commercial institutions** appeared on the scene; the latter provided finance, in particular, for the railway network.

- The **Swiss National Bank** (SNB) was created in 1907, long after the creation of the central banks of other European countries.

  For example: France, 1800; Austria, 1816; Germany, 1875; Italy, 1893.

- At the time the SNB was set up, there were some 450 banking establishments in Switzerland. Today, after many mergers and buy-outs, there are just over 300, among which are the two 'big banks': UBS and Credit Suisse. Both are in the spotlight, especially abroad.

The financial market place

- The success of a financial market place is linked to the **confidence** it inspires, especially when, as in Switzerland, its activities include the management of private fortunes; these activities are attractive to rich foreigners.

- In Switzerland, this confidence – always fragile – has been built up gradually. Two kinds of fundamental factors have determined its growth:
  – objective, such as the **strength of the currency**, banking professionalism, political **stability** and a sound legal framework (including, until recently, absolute **banking secrecy**);
  – symbolic, such as image and **reputation**; these are in part based on objective factors, but also include cultural and media elements, which is why banking is very sensitive to its image in the press and other media, including film.

International criticism

- As early as the inter-war period, the large Swiss banks were already being accused by the press and the French government of encouraging the flight of non-taxed foreign capital.

- At the end of the second World War, US newspapers criticised the involvement of Swiss banks in the Nazi war effort. They denounced the purchase of gold looted by the Nazis and the opening of bank accounts for the leaders of the Third Reich.

- In the 1950s and 1960s, Swiss banks were again attacked by the US government and press, who claimed that banking secrecy allowed the Soviet Union to use Swiss bank accounts to acquire controlling interests in industries of strategic interest to the USA.

- In the 1990s a major debate arose over **'dormant accounts'** and several Swiss banks were accused of failing to release to their heirs amounts held in the accounts of Jewish Holocaust victims.

In August 1998, UBS and Credit Suisse reached a settlement in a class action suit brought by Jewish associations in the USA, providing for the payment of $1.25 billion to Holocaust survivors and their legitimate heirs.

- Banking secrecy has been attacked in recent years by the tax authorities of the USA and some European countries, anxious to repatriate capital at a time of fiscal crisis.

SWISS BANKS

GOOD IMAGE
↓

BAD IMAGE
↓

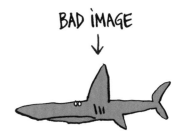

Banks in fiction

- The image of Swiss banking as a safe place to hide suspicious funds began to appear in post-war spy novels. It subsequently became a theme for films, television, comic books, etc.

One of the first appearances of a shady Swiss banker in film was in 1964 in 'Les Barbouzes' (The Great Spy Chase), a French production by Georges Lautner.

- A majority of James Bond films refer at some point to Swiss banks. In four of them, Swiss banking plays a central role.

Goldfinger, *1964;* On Her Majesty's Secret Service, *1969;* The World Is Not Enough, *1999; and* Casino Royale, *2006.*

During the 1950s and 1960s, there was fierce competition between the City of London and Zurich. The British accused the Swiss banks of weakening the pound Sterling. At this tense time, George Brown, the Labour Deputy Prime Minister, coined the phrase 'the gnomes of Zurich', which was rapidly taken up by the British press and is still used as a term of disparagement for Swiss bankers.

Punctuality

The clichéd image of the average Swiss combines punctuality with accuracy and imperturbability. The Swiss reputation for punctuality, with which a large part of the world is familiar, did not come about by accident; its origins lie in the history of the country and the development of its industrial activity.

Origins of the cliché

- In 1541, **Jean Calvin** published ecclesiastical decrees relating to the punctuality of the population of Geneva. They were, in particular, required to be at religious services on time subject to a monetary fine of three *sous*. In 1561, this policy was reinforced by new measures and clocks were installed across town to facilitate their implementation.

- Following Geneva's example, **public clocks** were mounted in other parts of Switzerland, and not only in the big towns. For example, when the French author and philosopher Montaigne passed through Basel in around 1580, he noted in his travel journal that every single small church had an impressive clock.

- When **tourism** began in earnest in the 19th century, the transport network comprised very different forms of conveyance (boats, stage coaches, the first trains, etc.). In order not to disappoint rich tourists, punctuality was essential to guarantee connections.

  The creation of a national railway network (serviced in the first instance by private companies, then – from 1902 – by the Swiss federal railways) reinforced the need to respect the timetable.

- In the 1940s, the **Swiss federal railways** commissioned an engineer, Hans Hilfiker, to design a new station clock. It had to be effective in ensuring that trains were on time while promoting the image of the operating company by associating it with punctuality.

  The special feature of this clock was its second hand, inspired by the small paddle-like baton used by Swiss stationmasters to signal the departure of trains: it paused briefly on the figure twelve and thus went round the clock face in less than 60 seconds.

For the Swiss federal railways, a train is considered on time if it is less than three minutes late.

- **Tourism** was not the only explanation for the renown of Swiss punctuality. It was also influenced by the development of watchmaking (····⇢ p. 88) and its reputation abroad.

  Expressions referring to Swiss punctuality or precision in several languages actually refer to Swiss watches, rather than to the Swiss themselves: e.g. 'runs like a Swiss watch' – 'come un orologio svizzero' – 'como un reloj suizo'.

The cliché spreads

The almost ritual reference to Swiss punctuality in tourist guidebooks provides an amusing indication of the spread of the cliché. Here are a few examples (translated from the original).

- *'The Swiss, manufacturers of the best watches in the world, are also renowned for their punctilious punctuality.'*
Le guide du Routard

- *'A Swiss will always arrive on time for a meeting.'*
Petit Futé

- *'If you are invited to a Swiss home, make sure you arrive on time; the punctuality of the Swiss is not a legend.'*
Guide Vert Michelin

- *'Short in speech, but righteous, the Swiss are very punctual.'*
Nouveau guide en Suisse, 1869

- *'The Swiss are unbeatable for punctuality.'*
Coup de baguettes sur la fourchette! Ou les Européens vus par un Chinois

- *'All modes of public transport are highly efficient, completely integrated, clean and usually punctual to the minute (among the most accurate clocks in Switzerland are those at railway stations).'*
Living and Working in Switzerland: a Survival Handbook

- *'If there is one virtue shared by all in Switzerland it is punctuality.'*
Passport Switzerland

- *'Swiss political stability is of great benefit to the prosperous banking sector. The country is known for its punctuality (everything is on time everywhere) and its cleanliness.'*
European Hunter

- *'The hotels are still comfortable and clean, the restaurants still excellent and welcoming, the trains still punctual and fast, and – most important – the people are still hospitable and courteous.'*
Fodor's

- *'We have lived in Switzerland and can vouch for the legendary punctuality of the Swiss.'*
Passports to Adventure

- *'As their name indicates, postal buses are operated by the postal services and are as punctual as the trains, making them a symbol of Swiss efficiency.'*
Central Switzerland: a Walking Guide

- *'Nevertheless, the Zurich public transport system is legendary: for its efficiency, for its punctuality and for its simplicity.'*
The Rough Guide

Swiss punctuality suffered a blow from the Japanese. *Collective Technology Corporation*, a company that analyses flight data for the aviation industry, gave number one ranking in punctuality to Japan Airlines in 2009 and 2010. For rail travel, the Japanese *Shinkansen* has a punctuality record that beats all-comers: in 2003, the average delay recorded for its entire network was six seconds.

Cleanliness

Like accuracy and punctuality, the cliché of cleanliness is a component of the Swiss 'quality label' and is put to profitable use by many products and services.

The myth and some statistics

- The myth of Switzerland's cleanliness is primarily linked to its urban environment: for many foreigners, even the sidewalks are immaculate.

- In environmental terms, cleanliness can also be measured statistically: the figures confirm the cliché.

A 2010 survey by Yale and Columbia universities placed Switzerland second only to Iceland in their Environmental Performance Index *covering twenty-two indicators, including air and water purity.*

A short history of waste management

- Between the 15th and 16th centuries, people were required to **sweep the space in front of their doors** as far as the centre of the street and then carry the sweepings to a central point. In the 18th century, this task was taken over by the municipal authorities.

- In 1904, Zurich was the first city to install a **waste incinerator**. Basel followed, but not until 1943; Bern and Lausanne were even later (in 1954 and 1958 respectively).

Plastic garbage bags were not in general use until the 1970s – until then trashcans were used. Today Switzerland sets a very good example by recycling more than 50% of its waste.

Swiss hotels

- In the 19th century, cleanliness was a **strong selling point** for Swiss hotels in attracting rich English tourists.

Edmond Guyer's 1877 work Les Hôtels Modernes *reported (translation): 'The real luxury of an English hotel lies in its perfect cleanliness; Swiss hotels apply the same policy .... which accounts in large part for their good reputation.' In 1913, Louis Farges, a French politician, described Swiss hotels in an article in the* Revue des deux mondes *(translation): 'After each guest has departed, not only is all the bed linen changed, but the floors and woodwork are carefully washed. Almost everywhere there are wash basins and toilets, all spotlessly clean.'*

'Clean as a Swiss whistle/sidewalk/street/ maternity ward/clinic/hotel/ chalet .....' – there is no shortage of expressions in English that repeat the cliché of Swiss cleanliness.

- This reputation was enhanced by the growth of **'health tourism'**, which required careful attention to hygiene and cleanliness.

Many tuberculosis patients, for example, went to sanatoria in the Swiss mountains for cures.

A cliché

- A concern for cleanliness forms part of the stereotype of the ordinary Swiss citizen and is often used in **fiction,** in satire and in popular jokes.

  There are frequent references to cleanliness in Asterix in Switzerland: *the hotel manager Petitsuix explains that a delegation of Barbarians has refused to take a room in his hotel because it was too clean for them. In Léa Fazer's 2004 film* Bienvenue en Suisse, *one of the characters drops an empty cigarette packet. Her Swiss friend picks it up and says: 'Please forgive her, she is French and, as you know, the French don't have garbage cans.'*

Irony

- Clichés provide fertile ground for **irony** in publicity and political slogans, as well as in the titles of books and articles.

  For his 1990 book on money laundering, Jean Ziegler chose the title La Suisse Lave Plus Blanc *(Switzerland Washes Whiter), applying the slogan for a detergent to the notion of 'dirty money', and managed to invert the stereotype of Swiss cleanliness.*

- The supposed contrast between a façade of cleanliness and certain hidden activities – shady and by implication 'dirty' – is regularly used in the international press when commenting on **scandals** involving Switzerland.

  In 2010, in his polemical article J'aime Polanski et je hais la Suisse *(I love Polanski and hate Switzerland), in the magazine* La Règle du Jeu, *Yann Moix wrote (translation): 'Everything is clean in the Swiss streets, in the Swiss mountains, in the Swiss valleys – everything is clean because, deep underground, in the foundations, in the basements, everything is filthy.'*

At the end of the 19th and beginning of the 20th centuries, showers were installed in several Swiss schools. The rules for their use included a requirement that all students should take a shower once a week.

I AM FIGHTING AGAINST THE CLICHÉ OF SWISS CLEANLINESS!

What makes it tick?

Such a simple question—"What makes it tick?"—that only a child can ask it. And only 300 years of Swiss watchmaking history can answer it.

For the heart of a really fine jeweled-lever Swiss watch is a miracle of precision wheels and gears that count off seconds, minutes, hours with fantastic accuracy. And to see behind the handsome dial is to marvel as much at your jeweler's knowledge as at the Swiss watchmaker's skill.

Your jeweler is an *expert* who can explain the perfection of workmanship that means the difference between Switzerland's finest jeweled-lever watches and all other watches. He'll show you how Swiss craftsmanship sets the world's standards of beauty, accuracy, value—as well as the standards of *ease, efficiency and economy of servicing.*

Only then will you understand exactly why *most* jewelers wear fine Swiss watches themselves.

For the gifts you'll give with pride, let your jeweler be your guide

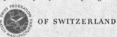

The WATCHMAKERS OF SWITZERLAND

© 1953 Swiss Federation of Watch Manufacturers

↑ **Banking** (Cartoon, 2003)

↖ **Watchmaking** (advertisement, 1953)
This advertisement by the Swiss watchmaking federation was published in the American magazine *Life*.

←← **Watchmaking** (prepaid telephone cards, 1997)
Prepaid telephone cards appeared at the end of the 1970s and were an important medium for images for some thirty years. The two shown here use imagery similar to that in the advertisement in *Life* magazine.

Institutions

The army

Although the Swiss army has never fought in a war, the fact that it is a militia means that it has been part of the daily life of generations of citizens.

From the cantons to the Confederation

- For a long time, the army was within cantonal jurisdiction. In 1848, the first federal constitution introduced compulsory military service and set in motion the centralisation of the army, an objective that was not finally achieved until **1874**.

- The length of the **initial phase** for training of recruits was extended and refresher courses were introduced (now every two years). Although the length of service has diminished in recent years, Swiss men are still required to spend a long time in the army.

A militia army

- The concept of the army as a militia, comprising citizen soldiers, typical of Switzerland, goes back to the Middle Ages. For both political and strategic reasons, it was adopted at the outset by the federal army.

General Herzog, elected during the Franco-Prussian war in 1870, considered that a professional army, smaller but smarter, would have been more effective.

Citizen soldiers

- Arms and uniform are provided by the Confederation and – as stated in Article 18 of the Constitution as early as 1874 – remain 'en mains du soldat' (in the soldier's possession). This provision, intended to permit rapid mobilisation, exemplifies more than anything else the image of the soldier-citizen.

In today's world, keeping a military gun at home has lost much of its military significance, but has powerful symbolic value. In February 2011, a referendum requiring military assault rifles to be returned and stored in a military depot was rejected by a 56.3% majority. The main poster used by opponents of the measure did not use military arguments but simply asked the question: 'Détruire les valeurs suisses?' ('Destroy Swiss values?')

In 1910, the Federal Council refused to finance the training of fighter pilots. In 1912–1914, the Swiss officers' association responded by raising 1.7 million Francs by public subscription (equivalent to 200 million at today's prices) for military aviation.

- Although there is a strong symbolic link between the people and the army, it has on several occasions been used against civilians, most notably in 1918 during the General Strike and in 1932 at a demonstration by the left against the far-right in Geneva: 13 demonstrators were killed and 65 wounded.

Marksmanship

- Keeping a rifle at home carried with it the requirement to use it regularly, not only during refresher courses, but also at compulsory annual **marksmanship practice**.

  Occasional marksmanship competitions for young people are also organised in various parts of the country. Both boys and girls, from the age of 10, are admitted.

- There are many **marksmanship associations**, some of them very old. Since the second half of the 19th century, they regularly organise **marksmanship festivals**. This is undoubtedly the reason why Switzerland was always among the leading countries in marksmanship at the Olympic Games of the early 20th century.

  In the 2008 Beijing Games, Switzerland did not win a single medal in this discipline.

- The importance of the marksmanship tradition is diminishing: during the Cold War, some 6000 military **shooting ranges** were available for compulsory target practice – now there are less than 1500. Of the 150,000 citizens called up for shooting practice, 10% prefer to pay a fine rather than participate.

Switzerland without an army?

- In 1982 a political association – *Groupe pour une Suisse sans Armée* (**GSsA**) – was set up to lobby for the reduction or even the elimination of public expenditure on national defence.

- The GSsA's first referendum in 1989 would have simply disbanded the army: it obtained 35.6% of the popular vote, a result that shook to its foundations the myth of a people at one with its army.

- The political fallout from this GSsA initiative brought a softening of military policy and, from 1992, exemption from military service on religious or political grounds was admitted. In the same year an alternative **'civic' service** was introduced, half as long again as military service.

  A survey undertaken in 2010 by the weekly magazine L'Hebdo *revealed that 43.5% of Swiss were in favour of compulsory military service.*

During the Cold War, one third of the budget of the Confederation was spent on the army. At that time, Switzerland had one of the numerically largest armies in continental Europe. Some 700,000 soldiers were operational, more than 10% of the whole population.

The Red Cross

The Red Cross is an international organisation, but its close association with its country of origin has given Switzerland the reputation of being a humanitarian nation.

Henry Dunant, founder

- Henry Dunant, a citizen of Geneva, was the founder of the Red Cross movement. While on a business trip to Italy in 1859, he was struck by the lack of care provided to the wounded at the battle of **Solferino**. He gave first aid to some of them and subsequently recounted his experiences in a book published in 1862, which created a sensation: *Un souvenir de Solferino* (A Memory of Solferino).

- In 1863, Dunant and four others – including General Dufour – set up the International Committee for Relief to the Wounded of War, which became the **ICRC** (International Committee of the Red Cross) in 1876.

Logo

- Dunant suggested that medical personnel should be given a neutral status to enable them to provide more effective assistance to the wounded – in other words, that they should not be fired on. This would require a distinctive emblem that would be easy to recognise and internationally acceptable. The Red Cross logo was designed for this purpose in 1863, even before the new organisation acquired its name. It inverts the colours of the flag of Switzerland, the neutrality of which had already been recognised.

The use of the logo by combatants is a war crime.

In 1922, China set up the Red Swastika Society, along the lines of the ICRC, using this ancient Buddhist symbol in place of the cross. The Society ceased operation in 1949.

In 1957, Sri Lanka requested ICRC permission to use this traditional symbol again; India did the same in 1977. Both requests were refused because of the association of the swastika with Nazi Germany.

- The **Christian symbolism** of the cross is a problem for some countries and a solution was found by recognising three alternative logos: the **red crescent** (suggested by Turkey in 1929), the combined red lion-and-sun (suggested in 1929 by Iran, although, after the Islamic revolution in 1979, it is no longer in use) and the red crystal (an all-purpose lay version, adopted in 2005, but rarely used).

The red star of David is used by Israel, but has not been officially accepted by the ICRC.

From humanitarian to medical use

- The red cross on a white background was rapidly adopted as a logo for medical establishments and products and as a badge for medical personnel, not necessarily related in any way to the ICRC.

- The red cross symbol rapidly gained international recognition. However, the ICRC denounced its use by pharmacies in many countries and the latter, forced to change their sign, managed to retain a visual resemblance either – as in France and Switzerland – in the form of a green cross, or – as in Germany – by keeping the same basic colours while replacing the cross with a capital 'A' (for *Apotheke*).

  In France, the use of a red cross by pharmacies was denounced in 1913. However, it was still in use by some as late as the 1950s.

Ambulances and first aid posts offering free treatment for the injured are permitted to use the Red Cross emblem. Most ambulances today bear the six-armed blue cross.

The Swiss humanitarian tradition

- A number of factors contributed to establishing the humanitarian tradition of Switzerland: the country's **openness to refugees**, beginning in the 16th century with the arrival of Protestant refugees from France, and, in the 19th, of political refugees; the creation of the Red Cross movement in Geneva; and the Swiss origin of a number of other **philanthropic organisations**.

  This reputation has been tarnished by the restrictive refugee policy of the country during the 2nd World War as well as by the number of recent referenda opposing the admission of refugees.

- The humanitarian tradition is a component of Swiss identity. As such, it cannot be ignored in the discourse of the political parties on the subject of refugees, even if the some of the measures proposed are restrictive in nature.

  In 2006, on the occasion of the referendum on the new national law on foreigners and asylum (considered one of the most restrictive in Europe), the right-wing member of the Federal Council, Christoph Blocher (UDC/SVP), stated: 'The partial revision of the law on asylum aims to preserve the Swiss humanitarian tradition while preventing abuse.'

Folklore

Folklore can be defined as a collection of popular traditions, normally linked to a region, but which, when combined, constitute a variegated and permanent image of a country.

SWISS BANKER
IN TRADITIONAL
COSTUME
↓

The Unspunnen stone, used during the first stone-throwing competitions, was kept at the Jungfrau Region Tourism Museum. In 1984, it was stolen by a group of Jura separatists who wanted a complete separation from the canton of Bern – for them, the stone was a symbol of the dominance of Bern over their region. It reappeared in 2001 at a festival in Saignelégier (canton of Jura) but disappeared again in August 2005.

Traditional costumes

- Traditional costumes are not of course specifically Swiss, but are found throughout Europe. Worn for festivals and processions, they are generally **specific to a region** (in Switzerland, to a canton); although, strictly speaking, they are not uniforms, they are made according to carefully regulated designs.

- The first costumes date back to the **18th century**, although, at the beginning of the 19th, they were abandoned in favour of garments more suited to urban living and which were considered more modern. They came back into fashion at the end of the 19th century, partly for **tourism** purposes, and then became part of national identity. In processions which show a couple from each canton, for example, they provide a good illustration of federalism.

Traditional costumes played an important role in almost all National Fairs.

National games

- In Switzerland, the national games are **Swiss wrestling** (commonly known as 'breeches-lifting' from the grip used by the wrestlers), **stone-throwing** and ***hornuss***, a kind of batting game in which one team attempts to use their bats to stop the flight of a puck hit by a member of the other team.

With the exception of hornuss, which is more recent, these games have been handed down from the competitions organised at popular sporting events since the end of the Middle Ages.

- In the mid-19th century, gymnastics (German or Swedish in origin) and some more modern sports of English origin (football in particular) grew in popularity; as a result, more emphasis was placed at official sporting events on the traditional games of Swiss origin on the ground that they were better adapted to inhabitants of the country.

- Today, these traditional games are still very much alive; there are 120 Swiss wrestling events every year and *hornuss* is played by 271 different teams.

Typical events

Several traditional events, originally regional in character, now belong
to national folklore:
- the **combat de reines**, typical of the canton of Valais,
  pits cows of the Hérens breed against one another;
- at carnival time in the Lötsch valley (canton of Valais),
  the *Tschägättä* – characters wearing hideous masks
  and animal skins – go through village streets ringing
  bells;
- the winemaking festival ('**Fête des Vignerons**'), organised once in a generation (1833, 1851, 1865, 1889,
  1905, 1927, 1955, 1977, 1999) by the winegrowers'
  brotherhood, mobilises virtually the whole population
  of Vevey (Vaud);
- the New Year is celebrated in the half-canton of
  Appenzell-Ausserrhoden with the *Silvesterklausen* –
  costumed characters wearing masks – who go from
  farm to farm ringing bells and singing a kind of yodel
  called a *Zauerli* to drive out evil spirits;
- *Poya* is the name given to the procession up to the
  summer meadows; in the Gruyère region, in particular, the *Poya* is
  the occasion for popular festivals of ancestral tradition.

TRADITIONAL 1ST OF MAY
DEMONSTRATION

The alphorn

- The alphorn is a powerful symbol of Swiss folklore. A wind instrument, generally made of spruce wood, it was originally used to
  communicate from one valley to another.

  There are similar instruments in Austria, Germany and France – and also in Poland,
  Ukraine and Romania.

- The instrument is usually 3.4 metres long, but can go up to
  18 metres.

  The most modern versions are made of carbon fibre and can be dismantled in
  sections for transport.

- Alphorn players regularly participate in all kinds of folklore events.
  They are among the figures that appear most frequently on postcards and tourist souvenirs.

Flag tossing is a game of skill
in which the participant
throws the flag in defined
aerial movements (there are
some fifty different ones); it
was brought back to Switzerland in the Middle Ages by
mercenaries who had served
in Southern Europe.

Swiss exceptionalism

Swiss exceptionalism – the Sonderfall in German – is a rather vague notion that Switzerland is a country different from all others, because of certain qualities it alone possesses.

THE SWISS ARE HARD-WORKING, ORDERLY, DISCIPLINED, PRECISE, HONEST PUNCTUAL, EFFICIENT...

...AND RATHER PROUD OF THEMSELVES!

Some electoral results, that may appear surprising to foreign commentators, have helped consolidate the myth of a country that is different. In 1985, for example, Swiss voters refused by a 65.2% majority to legislate a mandatory vacation of four weeks; and, in 2012, a 66.5% majority voted against a six-week vacation period. In 1988, an initiative to reduce the working week to 40 hours was also turned down by 65.7% of the electorate.

The cult of difference

- The notion of exceptionalism calls on Swiss **history** and **culture** to explain the peaceful coexistence of peoples with different languages and religions, living in a small geographical area, unravaged by wars and economically prosperous.

  Switzerland has only been multilingual since the 19th century. Until 1798, when the short-lived Helvetic Republic was proclaimed, the only language used for official purposes was German.

- Certain **virtues**, considered as typically Swiss, are taken to explain Swiss exceptionalism. The Swiss, according to the stereotypes, more than any other nation, appreciate work well done, carefully save their money, love cleanliness, have the gift of irreproachable honesty and demonstrate great accuracy in everything they do.

- This cult of 'being different', raised to the status of myth, sometimes becomes a kind of **ideology**, positing that approaches that are good for others are not good for Switzerland and that Swiss solutions are not applicable elsewhere.

The culture of consensus

- The Swiss consider themselves different from others, but are also characterised by diversity within their own frontiers. This **diversity** is **respected** at the level of national institutions – in the Federal Constitution, for example. The result is a culture of consensus that aims to resolve potential conflicts through the search for a compromise respecting all interests involved.

- The culture of consensus is valid not only in politics: in labour relations, a 1937 agreement between employers and trade unions, known as ***La paix du travail / Arbeitsfrieden*** (labour peace), obliges both parties to seek a negotiated solution to collective conflicts in the workplace. This agreement explains in part the very small number of strikes in Switzerland.

  It was not until the Federal Constitution of 1999 that the right to strike was recognised as a fundamental right.

Institutional exceptions

- The concept of Swiss exceptionalism reflects a wide variety of beliefs and ideas that are difficult to measure; it is given concrete form in very specific institutional arrangements.

- In politics, '**concordance**' is one expression of consensus. It consists in the search, before any major decision is taken, for negotiated solutions between the main parties and consultation of a wide range of interests, including economic and social groupings. A culture of '**collegiality**' in the decision-making of governmental authorities at all levels – communal, cantonal and federal – is one of the consequences.

The members of a 'collegial' government may belong to different parties, which are generally represented in proportion to the electoral votes each received. Moreover, no member of an executive has more voting power than the others.

- Although Swiss **federalism** is based on the US model, it is considered by almost all political parties as a fundamental feature of the Swiss system. It protects particularities and encourages proximity between citizens and the institutions of their canton, each of which has its own constitution.

One of the features of federalism is the requirement that all popular votes affecting articles of the Federal Constitution (whether by popular initiative or by referendum) must achieve a majority of votes across the whole country and a majority of cantons in favour.

- Together with federalism, **direct democracy** is the main characteristic of the Swiss political system. It implies regular and significant participation by citizens in decision-making. In addition to elections, familiar to all democracies, the Swiss are called to the polls three to eight times a year, not only to elect their communal, cantonal and federal authorities, but also to express their view on the many popular initiatives and referenda submitted for vote.

Even if participation in these various votes is not high in comparison with voting in other countries, direct democracy is very much part of national identity.

- Swiss **neutrality** (·····> p. 120) is also part of Swiss exceptionalism.

Since 1959, the composition of the Federal Council is determined by a so-called 'magic formula'. This practice, based on no written law, aims to form a government that includes representatives of the main political parties, thus ensuring their participation in decision-making and avoiding too frequent recourse to popular initiatives and referenda against government decisions. The representation in the Federal Council of the various linguistic regions of the country is, however, guaranteed by the Constitution.

↑↗ The army (posters, early 20th century and 1952)

The two faces of the citizen-soldier are shown here, in publicity as in politics.

→ The army (weekly magazine, 1938)

This cover from a Zurich magazine, a photomontage showing a Swiss soldier's head 'emerging' from the people, instrumentalises the citizen-soldier. The style resembles Soviet imagery of the same period. The characteristic shape of the helmet, adopted by the Swiss army in 1918 and in use until the 1970s, makes for easy recognition of the soldier as Swiss. This helmet became an integral part of military imagery for several generations, as can be seen from the 1919 commemorative medal shown below.

↑ **The Red Cross** (advertisement, late 19th century)

This advertisement uses the emblem and name of the Red Cross for the promotion of a Geneva pharmacy. There is of course a strong association of bandages with the image of the Red Cross, but such commercial use of the logo would be forbidden today.

→ **The Red Cross** (postcard, 1920s)

This card shows *Helvetia* next to a Red Cross nurse. The Swiss origin of the Red Cross emblem is reinforced by the 'mirror effect' of the crosses, as is the Swiss commitment to humanitarian activities at the time of the 1st World War, illustrated by the storm clouds in the background.

↑ Folklore (postcard, inter-war period)

The traditional costumes of the various cantons are shown across the map of Switzerland; in this way, the combination of regional particularities becomes a national symbol.

← Folklore (magazine, 1939)

This cover picture of *Der Schweizerische Beobachter*, a bi-weekly magazine, advertises the federal festival of Swiss wrestling and traditional games. This event, organised every three years since 1895 and still in existence, includes Swiss wrestling, *hornuss* and stone-throwing competitions.

↑ **Swiss exceptionalism** (poster, 1991)

On the occasion of the 700th anniversary of the Confederation, the University of Lucerne organised a colloquium with the title *Sonderfall Schweiz?* (Is Switzerland a special case?). This image, laden with symbols of identity – and including provocative images such as a nuclear power plant, barbed wire and a syringe, for example – is from the poster published for the event. Such an accumulation of images seems to be the only way to represent a concept as vague as Swiss exceptionalism.

External relations

Frontiers and the map of Switzerland

No nation can exist without a frontier ... The imaginary line that is a frontier results from long historical processes. The shape it gave to Switzerland was not always well-known to the population, but is the only genuine physical image of the country.

The determination of Swiss boundaries in lakes is not finally settled. For Lac Léman, the agreed boundary is in the middle, under a convention dating to 1564. For Lake Constance, however, there is disagreement: Switzerland considers that the frontier is on the median line, as in the case of Lac Léman; for Germany the lake is common territory; while for Austria it is no-man's-land.

What shape does Switzerland have?

- The present national frontiers were determined in **1815** at the Congress of Vienna, but some parts are older.

  The longest shared frontier is with Italy (744km), then France (572km), Germany (362km), Austria (180km) and Liechtenstein (41km).

- The shape of Switzerland does not bring to mind any specific configuration, such as the 'hexagon' of France or the 'boot' of Italy.

- It is only fairly recently that the Swiss population can be said to be familiar with the national map; this was the result of lessons learned during **compulsory schooling**, in force since the 1830s, although geography as a subject was not taught until the mid-19th century. From then on, the map of Switzerland became part of the perception of national identity and a symbol of the country.

  The first official map of Switzerland was commissioned by General Dufour. It was published in separate sections between 1845 and 1864. The oldest maps were not distributed widely – they were essentially for military purposes – and included unmapped regions, in particular in the mountains. The first university chair of geography was created in 1886 in Bern.

Is Switzerland an island?

- Even though Switzerland has no maritime frontiers, the country is often shown as an island in popular illustrations.

- The Swiss tradition of neutrality and Switzerland's refusal to join the **European Union** sometimes result in Switzerland being shown as a grey area on maps of Europe, but the metaphor of the country as an island is older.

  The image of the lake people (⋯⋯▸ p. 32) certainly plays a role in this perception: the platforms that were believed to have provided a home for these peaceful ancestors of the Swiss – and to have protected them from danger – feed the fantasy of Switzerland as an island.

- Island imagery was widely used during the two World Wars. Switzerland was often shown surrounded by tempestuous seas.

  In the somewhat simplistic imagery of postcards from the 1914–1918 period, the frontiers were often shown as a line between peace and the horrors of war, between well-being and poverty, between justice and barbarianism.

The frontiers as refuge

- Many films and novels – Swiss and foreign – contain scenes of crossing the Swiss frontier. In these works of fiction, soldiers, refugees, immigrants and escapees (including tax evaders) attempt to cross to reach a **safe haven**.

  Among the best-known films involving a frontier crossing into Switzerland: Jean Renoir's La Grande Illusion (1937), Léopold Lindtberg's The Last Chance (La Dernière Chance), 1945; Pietro Germi's The Path of Hope (Il Cammino della Speranza), 1950; and Markus Imhoof's The Boat is Full (La Barque est Pleine), 1981.

- As is frequently the case, fiction is founded on fact: many famous persons have found refuge in Switzerland – among others, the Italian patriot Giuseppe Manzini, the future Emperor **Napoleon III** (who even acquired Swiss nationality in the canton of Thurgau in 1832), the Russian revolutionary Vladimir Ilyich **Lenin** and the German philosopher Hannah Arendt.

Internal customs duties were levied in Switzerland until 1848. In 1844, Switzerland had more than 180 internal customs posts on cantonal frontiers, compared with only 147 on the external frontiers of the Confederation.

The closed frontier

- The image of Switzerland as a country of refuge is countered by that of 'fortress Switzerland', reflected in the words of Edouard von Steiger, member of the Federal Council who expressed the view in 1942 that the country could take in no more refugees by saying famously that '**the boat is full**'.

- Debates on asylum policy and on the expulsion of immigrants (reflected in the so-called **Schwarzenbach** initiative launched in the 1960s) sometimes create the image of a country that is hermetically closed or at least less welcoming than the more traditional version of a land of refuge.

  The poster published recently by the right-wing party SVP shows white sheep expelling a black sheep from Swiss territory – a contemporary image of a country that is no longer open.

Immigration and emigration

Immigration to Switzerland (as well as Swiss emigration abroad) has resulted in a cultural variegation that has changed the image Switzerland has of itself and has reinforced this image abroad.

Immigrants

- Prior to the 19th century, there were few foreigners in Switzerland. The **first wave** resulted from political unrest in Europe. After the failure of the bourgeois revolutions of **1848** in neighbouring countries, more than 100,000 refugees fled to Switzerland.

- The **second wave** – driven this time by employment – arrived forty years later and was the result of the major works undertaken for railway construction (⟶ p. 70), which brought some 260 000 workers to Switzerland between 1888 and 1910. The first **Italian** immigrants arrived at this time.

- Between the 1st and 2nd World Wars, immigration dropped and it was not until the return of economic growth in the **1950s** that it picked up again. Between 1951 and 1970, 2.68 million foreigners came to Switzerland, most of whom were **seasonal** workers in the **building** industries and the **restaurant and hotel** business; their work permit did not allow either permanent residence or family reunification.

  From 1962, in addition to Italians, many immigrants came from Spain; then, from 1980, from Yugoslavia, Portugal and Turkey.

- Immigrant workers contributed to the evolution of the image of Switzerland, and also to the awareness abroad of Swiss culture, through contact with their families during the holidays and when they finally returned home.

Between 1960 and 1980, some 5 million Italians came to Switzerland as labour migrants, 1 of every 15 Italians of this generation.

- In the 1970s, Switzerland was perceived as a country of immigration, an *Eldorado* with zero unemployment.

  The well-known Italian film Pane e cioccolata (Bread and chocolate), *produced by Franco Brusati in 1972, tells the story of an Italian immigrant in the German part of Switzerland. This meeting of two worlds was perceived at the time as a real culture shock.*

Xenophobia

- Contrary to popular perception, immigrants are well represented in professions requiring a high level of qualification. In 1951, for example, more than 40% of scientists active in the private sector in research and economic development were foreigners. The most 'visible' immigrants in real numbers (in the sense that there are more masons than scientists) have low-qualified jobs.

- Immigrants are essential for the development of the economy. However, since the late 19th century, they have been **viewed negatively** by some Swiss.

In 1893 and 1896 there were riots against Italian immigrants in Bern and Zurich.

- This negative attitude to foreigners led to the creation of xenophobic political parties, such as *Action nationale* in 1961 (renamed *Démocrates suisses* in 1990). Between 1965 and 1988, six citizens' initiatives for the reduction of so-called '**foreign overpopulation**' were launched, but all were rejected.

In 1971, the PAI (Party of peasants, artisans and independents) merged with other small parties to form the SVP. This new grouping subsequently promoted several new initiatives against immigration, right of asylum and simplified naturalisation.

The fifth Switzerland

- Switzerland has been home to many immigrants, but there are also many Swiss who have sought their fortune abroad.

- Between 1870 and 1914, the population of Switzerland grew from 2.65 million to nearly 4 million. This demographic explosion led many inhabitants to emigrate.

- In the 19th century, the US government encouraged immigration to aid in industrialisation and economic development. The Swiss were considered as 'good immigrants' and had no problems settling in.

Some 1.2 million Americans are of Swiss origin.

- Today, more than **732,000 Swiss** (most with dual nationality) live abroad. This community makes up the 'fifth Switzerland' in addition to the four linguistic communities of the country.

France has the most Swiss inhabitants, followed by Germany, the USA and Italy.

In the USA, more than 5000 towns have Swiss names: Geneva – 26; Zurich – 4; and Lucerne – 18.

Mercenaries

Mercenary service has a long tradition in Switzerland. This could be embarrassing for a country whose identity is founded on neutrality, but this is not the case.

THE JOB OF POPE'S GUARD IS NOT DANGEROUS...

...UNLESS RIDICULE CAN KILL!

In the early 16th century, representatives of 'reformed' religion began to oppose mercenary service. Ulrich Zwingli of Glaris was one of the leaders of this movement. According to some historians, one of the reasons why the original Swiss cantons remained Catholic was because they did not want to give up the rich rewards from foreign mercenary service.

A long-standing tradition

- Mercenary service goes back to antiquity, but the golden age for Switzerland was between the 16th century Italian wars and the French Revolution.

- Mercenary service abroad was contrary to the **principle of Swiss neutrality** enshrined in the first Federal Constitution of 1848. However, a law was passed permitting the fulfilment of contracts already concluded and allowing individual service. In 1859, finally, the authorisation of the Federal Council was required for professional engagement in military activity abroad.

The Swiss guards

- The Swiss guards were **elite mercenaries** whose task was to protect a sovereign and the sovereign's representatives.

  The pay of a Swiss guard was higher than that of ordinary mercenaries.

- The oldest and best known mercenary guard company is the ***Cent-Suisses*** (Hundred Swiss) established in 1497 by the French king Charles VIII. Disbanded during the Revolution, it was reinstated by Louis XVIII in 1814 and lasted until 1830.

  Similar companies served in Sardinia, Tuscany, Austria, Brandenburg and the Papal States.

The Vatican guards

- Founded in **1506**, at the height of the military prowess of Swiss mercenaries, the Vatican guards are the sole mercenary company still serving today.

  The present uniform, similar to the one worn during the Renaissance, was introduced in 1914. It has made the Swiss guards one of the major tourist attractions in Rome.

- Comprising some **hundred** Catholic soldiers under the command of a colonel – traditionally from Lucerne – the Vatican guards are today the only military forces of the Vatican.

  The Swiss guards have symbolic value for the Vatican, but also for Switzerland. Their international visibility is very important and they recall the positive aspects of Swiss mercenary service.

'Red Gold'

- From the late Middle Ages, mercenary service was taken in hand by the authorities. The cantons concluded contracts with kings and kept part of the fees.

- Mercenary service had significant economic and social effects. Firstly, the **monetary rewards** for the cantons (and for the troop commanders) were high, to the point that people spoke of 'red gold' in reference to the blood shed in mercenary activity. In addition, the **emigration** that resulted from mercenary service absorbed part of the inactive population.

Today it might be said that it was a measure for reducing unemployment.

'Honour and loyalty'

- The reputation of mercenary service has **improved** since the beginning of the 20th century. Previously, the hundreds of thousands of Swiss bearing arms for money were relegated to the darker chapters of Swiss history.

- From 1910, the works of Paul de Vallière gave Swiss mercenary service a firm place in national mythology. Specific events – such as the Tuileries massacre in 1792 or the rescue of the Pope during the sack of Rome in 1527 – were idealised in a way that exalted the courage, the honour and the loyalty of Swiss mercenaries abroad. These virtues were praised for themselves, irrespective of the power that they served.

Relics

- The **Lion of Lucerne** monument, carved from solid rock in 1821, commemorates the Swiss guards who perished in the fall of the Tuileries in 1792.

- During the Corpus Christi festival (*Fête-Dieu* in French) in the Lötsch valley in the canton of Valais, the **'Grenadiers du Bon Dieu'** parade in antique uniforms. The tradition goes back to the time when men from this region went for service abroad. Some of them, in particular those who had been in the service of the kingdom of Naples, kept their parade uniform to wear at religious festivals.

Swiss mercenaries faced each other in battle only rarely. However, it happened in 1709 at Malplaquet during the Spanish War of Succession: the Swiss were enrolled in the forces of both the French and the coalition under Anglo-Dutch leadership. 8000 Swiss died on both sides.

Neutrality

Switzerland's 'neutrality in perpetuity' was recognised by the Congress of Vienna in 1815. The 1848 Federal Constitution made neutrality a central feature of Swiss foreign policy.

The word 'neutrality' comes from the Latin words *ne* and *uter* – 'neither one nor the other'.

The tradition of 'good offices'

- The services that Switzerland is able to render during conflicts provides a concrete illustration abroad of Swiss neutrality.

  These services include asylum, mediation between belligerents, hosting international conferences and humanitarian assistance.

- The 1870 Franco-Prussian war was fought close to the frontiers of the Confederation. The Federal Council then added 'good offices' to its policy of neutrality, including, for example, the **diplomatic representation** of States at war and the **internment** of combatant units that had withdrawn to Swiss territory.

  The treatment given in 1871 to the troops of the French General Bourbaki has become famous.

- A policy based on 'good offices' follows logically from the foundation of the **Red Cross** in 1863, and from the first **Geneva Conference** in 1864, which laid the groundwork for humanitarian rules applicable in armed conflicts.

Neutrality and national cohesion

- The cultural, linguistic and religious differences within Switzerland may give the impression that its internal cohesion is fragile. Although neutrality is part of foreign policy it is also an internal unifying factor.

  During the 1st World War, for example, alignment with one or other of the belligerents could have had major internal repercussions. The French- and Italian-speakers were more in favour of France, Italy and their allies; the German-speakers more for Germany and Austria.

- Swiss neutrality has not always been followed with the same rigour, especially in cases where important economic and other interests were at stake. Arms sales and financial transactions are typical cases in which strict neutrality was breached.

  During the Cold War, Swiss foreign policy was marked by a determination to maintain strict formal neutrality, even though the country was clearly aligned – economically and politically – with the Western powers.

Armed neutrality

- Neutrality should not be confused with pacifism, even less with anti-militarism. Throughout its history, the Confederation has always maintained a strong army and has devoted major resources to defence. One of the reasons was the prohibition of military alliances, even of a defensive nature. Thus, ideally, Switzerland should be able to ensure the defence of its territory on its own.

League of Nations and UN

- Switzerland's reputation for neutrality explains the choice of **Geneva** for the headquarters of the newly formed League of Nations in 1919.

In 1920, Swiss voters approved membership of the League by a majority of 56%. The federal government accepted the obligation to apply economic sanctions decided by the member States, but could opt out of any military sanctions.

- After the 2nd World War, Swiss neutrality was not viewed favourably by the victors and Switzerland was not invited to the founding conference of the United Nations (which replaced the League of Nations). The **Palais des Nations** in Geneva, former headquarters of the League, became the European Office of the United Nations, second only to the New York headquarters.

After many years of Swiss absence from the UN, membership was put to popular vote in 1986 but was rejected by 75% of the electorate. In 1994, 57% of voters rejected Swiss participation in UN peacekeeping forces. Swiss UN membership was finally approved by the people in 2002, by a majority of 54.6%.

In 1999, during NATO operations in Yugoslavia – which did not have a UN mandate – Switzerland observed strict neutrality and did not grant overflight permission to NATO fighter planes. However, despite the fact that the country had not yet joined the UN, the government did apply sanctions against Iraq in 1991, as they had been formally endorsed by the UN.

↑ Frontiers and the map of Switzerland (postcard, 1915)

On this card, the outline of Switzerland delimits an area of peace amidst the hell of war. At the centre, a character halfway between *Helvetia* and Heidi is looking down from her mountain retreat at the misery all around.

← Frontiers and the map of Switzerland (postcard, 1917)

Here Switzerland is turned into an 'island of peace', protected from the surrounding tempest. The lighthouse at the centre radiates the humanitarian values of the country in time of war (internment of wounded prisoners of war, care of refugees, information on missing persons, etc.).

↓↘ Immigration and emigration (posters, 1920s and 1960s)

On these two xenophobic posters, the image of a frontier about to be violated is exploited to alert voters to the 'danger' of immigration.

↑ **Mercenaries** (painting, early 20th century)

The painter Karl Anneler depicts a 'grenadier du Bon-Dieu' (····⟩ p. 119) in the uniform worn at the time of mercenary service abroad.

↗↗ **Mercenaries** (photo, 1955; and sculpture, 1821)

Two other reminders of the 'mercenary' period: a parade in mercenary uniform by the 'Cent-Suisses' association (····⟩ p. 118) at the 1955 Fête des Vignerons (····⟩ p. 105); and the Lion of Lucerne monument erected in memory of the Swiss mercenaries killed in the 1792 Tuileries massacre (····⟩ p. 119).

↓ **Neutrality** (postcard, 1914)

Neutrality is guaranteed by Helvetia, the army and the frontiers, and preserves Switzerland from the horrors of war.

Index

Index

More books about Switzerland

www.bergli.ch

Swiss History in a Nutshell
by Grégoire Nappey,
cartoons by Mix & Remix

Bergli Books,
ISBN 978-3-905252-19-4

Swiss Democracy in a Nutshell
by Vincent Kucholl,
cartoons by Mix & Remix

Bergli Books,
ISBN 978-3-905252-63-7

**Beyond Chocolate –
understanding Swiss culture**
by Margaret Oertig-Davidson

Bergli Books,
ISBN 978-3-905252-21-7

**Hoi – your new Swiss German
survival guide**

Bergli Books,
ISBN 978-3-905252-67-5

**Hoi Zäme – Schweizerdeutsch
leicht gemacht**
by Sergio Lievano and
Nicole Egger
(for German speakers)

Bergli Books,
ISBN 978-3-905252-22-4

**Hoi! Et après... Manuel de
survie en suisse allemand**
by Sergio Lievano and
Nicole Egger
(for French speakers)

Bergli Books,
ISBN 978-3-905252-16-3